# POMES

*P. Osito*

Collected Poems and Prose 1998 - 2002

Supposed Crimes, LLC • Matthews, North Carolina

All Rights Reserved
Copyright © 2017 P. Osito

Published in the United States.

ISBN: 978-1-944591-38-0

www.supposedcrimes.com

This book is typeset in Goudy Old Style.

Author's Note: Even though the distance of time cannot be understated, more of these were written with the vague notion of "better out than in" in whatever respect you may wish to place upon it.

1. 1998.01.03

This book of horrors that
one unlocks
unbarring all within
for the sun dares not to shine
down onto
all those covered with sins.

Dark it remains,
in the farthest of corners
and dark it will be,
for no mortal eyes should look
upon the immortal souls of
these.

Flee away from these souls
forlorn,
I do not want to see your scorn,
for your pity and your
compassions
tears me apart
and brings no comfort
to this unfeeling heart.

2. 1998.06.17

Life and Death are delicately
balanced upon a blade.

A life that is not my own,
is not worth living.

3. 1998.06.29

How fleeting life is,
like a candle
that flickers in the wind.

Madness is not the ledge
that I have descended upon,
but the cloak that hides
the great unhappiness that I feel.

Slowly I drop,
further into the despair
that has become me.

Or perhaps it is depression.

I can seek no solace for there is
no shelter for the sinner.


4. 1998.06.29

Be still,
and the beat slows ~
soon a river of red will flow
and look to that day
where my past
no longer haunts me
where happiness is
a road to travel.

Soon comes the day of
release, relief and rejoicing.
No longer will I be both
the bearer and the scorned.

## 5. Signs of Loss - 1998.07.11

Cynicism is usually the first sign.

Then it is a recession
into a formal persona which
includes formal diction and
nuances.

Then one observes a 'distancing'
of the
patient from surrounding peers
~ an isolation phase

Finally, absolute isolation is
intertwined
with a delusional mode of
thought.

Depression ~ is that the word
that I am looking for?

Cynicism ~ is that what I really
feel?

My dishonourable actions
reflect upon the honour and
reputation of my friends
~ better if I do not cast
my shadow upon their light.

## 6. 1998.07.11

Hollow, hollow -
that is what I feel -
a vessel of emptiness
that would sooner overflow
with the bitterness
that overwhelms me.

If I were to go,
I don't believe too many
would mourn the loss -
for it would be a removal
of the blight
that tarnishes the shine
upon their honour.

It is not really a loss -
perhaps better seen as a release
from this cell
that is the invisible prison
of my life.

Without honour, I am nobody,
risen from the dust,
as Adam's child, I return.

Soon, that day comes
when this frail body
becomes one with the earth -
and the soul, my soul!
will leave
to embark on the journey
beyond living.

And that day will be
a day of joy - no longer
of pain.

I look to that time,
with great yearning
and anticipation.

I put back my feelings
into that box of ice -
better not to feel anything
than to constantly face pain.

The pain draws my attention
away from the fear,
the hate,
the cold that exists
in my life.

Pain dulls your sense
to all others -
to watch life
through a hazy window
that cannot look away.

# 7. Falling - 1998.07.11

Falling
falling
into the welcoming arms of
darkness
~ how soothing it is
everything is placed within
a box like
an automaton - unfeeling,
unthinking.

And so I am
like a Russian doll
one within another
our faces painted smiles,
our insides empty
holding nothing
but meaningless
memories.

And the world continues to spin,
regardless of the time,
there is no rest for the sinner

Oh how weary I am.

I am my own burden,
walking through
this endless path
of unceasing despair.

There are days that I dream ~
how fleeting mine are,
of a life without pain
almost doll-like in nature,
but I know
it is only
a false image
that tantalizes and
teases my soul.

Dancing towards and
then away from my outstretched
fingers,
this faint hope
dims
as my eagerness
vanishes in time.

Darkness looms over me.

Once, I will embrace its
warmth and bid
a quiet farewell
to this world.

The few that knew me,
would shed some tears,
but this final act
of redemption
should give me
in death what I could
not have in life.

## 8. Emptiness - 1998.07.11

The emptiness that engulfs me,
that roils and turns over
like a restless beast from
the depths of darkness.

I feel nothing: no joy,
no sorrow ~ no feeling
but this soul-wrenching
emptiness.

I will sooner kill myself
than reveal this terrible face to
the world.

My anger,
rumbled in a urge
for release but
I cannot let it go.

It protects me
from the hurt that would
surely follow upon the
feelings of defeat.

I must school myself ~
say nothing, express nothing,
just do.

Every time
that I have said something,
I received nothing
but defeat in return.

Every time
that I have expressed something,
I have received only
scorn and mockery.

This has come to an end,
I exist no longer.

From this day forth,
I no longer walk
upon this Earth.

The soul that once was,
has left the husk
that held it.

No one mourns the loss
of something that never was.

Do not mourn my loss
for I have set myself
free.

The soul, if not the body,
has joined within
the greater Dance of Life.

No more does it
limit itself to a frail
corpse that could not
dance.

## 9. Trains - 1998.07.11

one
two
three
how neatly my lines
arrange themselves.

I want to see the railroads
that run across
expanse of pale flesh.

Throbbing red and blue,
a steady beat
against the surface.

How often does the train run ?
It's never quite on time.

Some days, it runs more often,
others, it comes not at all.

Who runs the train ?
Is it fate ? Or is it man ?

I really cannot tell you;
I can't see a light
at the end of this tunnel,
maybe it's too dark.

This train runs on
a downhill slope,
it does not travel upwards.
The ride is always
down
down
down.

can you buy a ticket ?
I'd rather you did not,
there are no stations
from here to there
~ just a trip filled
with good intentions.

Tell me who the conductor is,
is it really you ?

The conductor is not the
engineer,
the conductor is not on the
train.

Are there any passengers
on board
for this trip to Hell ?
I really cannot say;
there's no way to tell.

It starts in Life
and ends in Death,
is that not enough ?

No windows for the scenery,
no bunkers for a rest,
this trip to Hell is
now Express
and does not stop along way.

So when the trip ends
with the train meeting the end
of
its tunnel,
I suspect there
is no turning back.

There is no return fare
no chance to turn around,
The train has stopped
simply because
it has run aground.

## 10. Heart - 1998.07.11

So much poetry
fills these pages
pouring out
my heart.

My heart is empty,
nothing shines,
nothing light.

Wrench it out ~
the pain
is too much to bear.

Take the wretched organ
and still the pulsing beat.

Draw breath no more,
draw in the last
remnants of happiness
in your memories.

Hold them dear;
for they are in the past
and there is no future
that I can see.

## 11. Woe - 1998.07.19

Once upon a time,
there was a family
of a mother, father
and three happy children.

It was many years ago,
once upon a time,
the tale is old,
the story past
and the children
happy no more.

When did this tale of woe
began, I really cannot say.
All I know is that
the magic's gone
and we have no ending at all.

## 12. Salt - 1998.07.19

A slight tang of salt
sequestered in a tear
lick the drop away
hold it very dear

The hollow feeling
pings against
the emptiness that once was

The thumping sound
of blood in veins
rocks
then stops.

## 13. Pandora's Box - 1998.08.08

The mind is a Pandora's box
chock full of emotions
with the carelessness
of a hint
emotion is released

Slowly
it drips
onto our consciousness
and flows
blood red
through my eyes

And if I could
I would go back to
that day
to never have opened
that box.

## 14. 1998.08.08

Warmth
lies in the light
just as despair
surrounds us

The happiness of living
holds the sorrow
at bay

But does it really?

Darkness holds us enthralled
enchanted by its sheer power

Squeezing
squeezing
my soul
pulses slowly
and does not struggle
against the warmth
of
the
darkness.

## 15. Ask - 1998.08.08

People often wonder why do I
indulge upon the forbidden ~
why do I immerse myself in
my anime, my fan-fiction,
my comics or my 'interests'
as they were.

I cannot tell them that
this is Escapism at its max.

People often ask me why do I
act so anxious to see others
happy

and I cannot tell them
that that is the only moment
where I can see ~ happiness
for there is none in my own life

And people ask: why are you so
formal

and I cannot tell them
that this keeps them safe ~
from my pain,
my anger,
my failures in the world

and they ask: why not let go of
the anger

and I cannot say
on with anger and despair
do I still know
that I am living

And people ask: what are your
dreams

and I cannot answer;
those without feeling
cannot dream

Once I dreamt of life
beyond the first quarter

but now, I don't think
that my parents should
seek children of my body ~
such is the chilliness
that freezes my soul
~ eternally captive in
a frozen state

I can only imagine their
shock
anger
disbelief
to hear that their daughter
is not normal but ____
but perhaps it is better
that I seek love
elsewhere
than believed

Bondmates and childmates
to borrow words from Herriot
~ something I cannot seek.

## 16. Wine - 1998.10.04

This wine of
bitterness
that flows within the soul
slowly travels
from heart
to throat
to mind

There is no real
answer to this thirst
of bitterness
that has
bitten me

Free will has
long since been
something
that I dream of
but do not hope for

Attempts to assert
oneself
are as futile
as ice on
a warm
summer's day

One day
it will come to an end
where all things sought
are found

Where freedom
of the soul
is found from
without
as the spirit
slowly
drifts away.

## 17. Ice - 1998.02.18

Ice
is it possible to feel
so cold inside
that nothing
shows without?

Is it possible to
freeze all your
emotions
yet
live without?

There is a wall of ice
that surrounds me
holding a-bay
that which would
probably kill me...

Ice
is what keeps me alive
yet deadens me inside;
if you cannot feel,
you cannot hurt,
you cannot weep,
and most importantly,
you survive.

Surviving
is not living,
that is something else
altogether.
Surviving
is living
without
hope.
without
love.
without

life.

There is this fist
that clenches
around my heart
what little left there is...
it clenches each time
to ensure that
I continue
to breath
to see
but
not to live.

Ice
is the only shelter I have
against the winds
buffet around me.
It is the shield that
would make me and
break me in the same day
- shelter against the winds
but leeching my meager life.

Ice is the one constant
in my days;
none other can pierce so cleanly
the frail bit which is my soul.

Water is soft
yet hard at the same time
for does it not form ice?
and does it not surround you
with warmth
and coldness
at the same time?

Ice
is the only anchor
within the ocean
of emotions
that I travel
that I have
that I end with.


## 18. Numb - 1999.05.21

Numbness.

Standing stock still
a reddened print on the side
numbly watching

welcome
into my heart
the pain
that assaults me

embrace it
like an old friend
the only
friend
I've ever known.

I am numb.

## 19. Rules – 1999.07.16

1. Loneliness is your friend. Do not lose sight of your isolation.
2. No feelings. No pain. Feel nothing. Want nothing.
3. The pain assaults you, embracing like an old friend. The only friend ever known.
4. Your goal is to survive. Survive from minute to minute. From second to second. From day to day.
5. Remember nothing. Feel nothing. Say nothing.
6. Silence is a gift. Treasure it.
7. The ice that surrounds you is a shelter. Face away from the world.
8. Live in the now. There is no future.
9. Reveal nothing. Revel in nothing.
10. Forget your past. Tabula rasa.

## 20. 1999.08.21

When they say that love hurts,
I don't believe that they were
describing a physical pain.

Well... it is a physical pain,
a fist that clenches your chest
and squeezes.

## 21. 1999.09.04

There is a hole that exists
in the center of my soul -
my heart is empty,
my soul unfulfilled.

There is an emptiness that
pervades my life
- a barrenness that lives within me
- a lifelessness that begets naught
- a sullenness that reads like whitenesss
- a tundra of confusion
that is endless.

## 22. 1999.09.04

My sins are catching up to me,
surely and slowly
I am confronted
by the ideal
and my flaws show up.

I cannot hide
from the mirror
where eyes not my own
look out
onto me.

Where lives not lived
fill my book.

Where love is a barren thought
and hate the dominant trait.

I wait
for the day
where I will be free
to live
to die
to love
to hate
to feel something
I have not felt in twenty years.

## 23. 1999.09.04

I am
a canvas
tattered and torn
no longer
the pure colour
I was.

All my mistakes are here
all my faults are here
all the attempts
and failures
are here
there is no image here
that I can see.

## 24. 1999.09.04

To treasure the days
that once were
I keep

a calendar -
when I might has seen a movie
when I might have had a lunch
when I might have enjoyed a day
and I treasure these days
because I can count them
on two hands
but never three
and never again.

I have four, no five
of such calendars
each year
carrying the days
that I might have lived
a day or two

My days are filled now
with mindless work
with thoughtless chores
that fill but do not sustain.

My mind struggles
to not think,
just do,
don't feel,
just do,
don't talk,
just do,
don't emote,
just do.

To not feel - the ultimate in
protections;

to not emote - the utmost in
skill.

I too, look towards the day
where I can leave the life
that is my sham
the hoax that has lasted
for so long.

There comes a time
where I won't be needed,
hated, loved, or sought
- I am waiting for that day.

So that my relief will
be palpable
and my sorrow
intangible.

I am waiting.

I will be patient.

## 25. 1999.09.04

The disappointment
is a tangible bitterness
on my tongue.

The hatred
that fills their eyes
batters against
the isle that is
me.

To mingle with the shrieks
of an albatross
that is stranded here.

On the desert island
that resembles no paradise,
there is no message in the bottle
no hope for redemption,
there is no escape.

## 26. Time - 2000.03.06

Time is fleeting when she is
here...
as is all things...
time is relative when she's not
here.
for that which we wait...
time stretches to an unbearable
length
as the grains of time slowly sink
yet, when you are together
there is never enough time,
for it speeds and slows

## 27. Dark Souls - 2000.03.06

we are all dark souls
waiting for the light to find us
or we to find them
so that their light
may burnish away our pain
yet never dim their joy
for no one should go throughout
life
without their light.

## 28. Thorns - 2000.03.06

The path of thorns
is strewn with rocks
and as we tread carefully
amongst the stones
we avoid those that we feel
would hurt us
both the joy
and the pain
that makes us grow
and so it is,
that we try
to lead safe lives
that are sterile in comfort
and cool in reality
such that we miss
those that would love us
and lead us through
till the end of days.

## 29. Ironic – 2000.03.07

Is it not ironic
to believe in soulmates
but never find your own?

To realize that
halves
are not always halves
and a peg
in a square hole
still does not fit

To watch
in a detached manner
that all of those
around you
are happy
which lends
a measure
of satisfaction
but know that
you return to
no place
that is
home

For your soul
is not there,
but out
seeking one
to complete
the puzzle.

## 30. Isolation – 2000.03.07

The emptiness that surrounds
me
protects me from the pain;
with no love
there are no feels
of happiness,
joy,
pain,
loneliness.

There is no fear
of the future
nor the past
that binds me tightly
to the road.

The road I travel
is a lonely one
with no signs
nor
travelers
along the way.

## 31. Cold - 2000.03.07

It is cold comfort that I take
to know that I am
searching
for the light
that is my soul.
One that would
quench my thirst for love
such that my spirit tires
in the struggle.

To know that there -is- a one
meant for me
that accepts me
as I am
as I was
as I will be.

It is with cynical grace
that I live
withdrawn from life
but for a bar
where I write
to drown my sorrows.

It is with futility
that I search
for that other half
of the soul -
a treasure beyond price
to be held carefully
for they would
hold my heart
and cleave my soul.

It is the lingering pain
of the fear
that binds me tightly
and carefully.

## 32. 2000.03.12

There is a certain sense
of perversity
held against lovers
such that
their fates suffer
both in the throes of passion
and the entanglement of pain.

The inability to stop
loving makes us
so vulnerable
that it almost
seems more desirable.

## 33. Satin - 2000.04.13

There is the tantalizing feel of
satin
sliding across your skin
carefully
drifting
across
the
peaks
and valleys
that shelter the sweet taste
of
your
body.

## 34. One – 2000.04.15

One is the number
that separates the near from the
far.

One day –
for every day that separates
them,
one day is too long
every day that is between
feels like a year
a lifetime
many lifetimes.

One day –
for every day that they are
together,
it is never enough
every day passes too quickly
each memory is a lifetime
each moment is a treasure

One separates
the other…
by virtue
of distance
of age
of time

## 35. Moon – 2000.04.26

The moon
three thousand miles
across the land

the moon rises
and a lonely heart
offers her thoughts
to the moon
in hopes that
the one she loves
will, too,
look to the sky
and think of her

Separated
by time
and distance
the two lovers
love apart

sharing with the moon
their deepest thoughts.

## 36. Colours – 2000.04.29

The colours of love
are such that it runs
beyond 256 and more than
100,000

for the colour is blue
when you cannot find it
and a pale pink
of the first blush

it is the yellow sunshine
that fills your day
and the black of the nights
you share

it is the millions of shades
of grey
that lie between
yes
and no

it is the green of the envy
you feel
and the diamond clear tears
when she cries

it is the red
that marks the anger
of the first argument
and the light blue
when she forgives you

grey is the colour
that represents us both best;
a mixing of two lives
and two hearts.

it reminds me of the mist
just before the dawn
and the subtle shadows
that fill the room
we share

and flesh is the colour
as I feel your skin
against mine
flushed pink with exertion
and our cheeks
turn a soft rose
the first time our eyes meet
even as our souls
have communicated
beyond
like
the colours of the sky

red marks the first roses you give
and aqua are your eyes
as your flush
becomes
a swirl
of colours.

## 37. Awakenings - 2000.04.30

The morning mist that lies
lightly over the land shimmers
as I watch you
in the early hours of the day

I trace the sharp contours
softened by sleep
with my eyes,
as I so often do
in the wee hours of the day

Always
in awe of this gift
you've given,
something beyond price
and treasured like a dragons gold

Slowly the sun rises
and with it,
the last vestiges of sleep
are washed away.

As the sunrise warms the air
I watch you stretch
angling your arms just so
around me
enfolding me in your love

It is a luxurious feel,
to be wanted,
for naught than
being myself

I forget my worries and sorrows
concentrating only on you
the one other even in my life
that captivates my attention
so completely
that I forget myself.

## 38. Ambrosia - 2000.05.02

There is a certain piquancy in
love,
to have tasted it once,
is like ambrosia,
to live without -
sweet torture.

Having only eaten gruel
for so long,
the taste of honey -
can never be erased;
it lingers long after
its gold drops are
treasured.

Like a delicacy
one would be so lucky
to visit
that candy store
where this golden treat
is kept.

So well hidden
that we are never entirely sure
that we are looking
for the real thing.

Too often
do we deny ourselves
and others
the sweet taste
of this joy,
because we've never seen it,
never sought it.

-title by KS

## 39. Dark Soul - 2000.05.02

Sitting in the dark
I see so clearly
the outlines of the
things that lie
in my room.

The pale moonlight shines
casting a hazy sheen
on all that is below.

Struggling to peer
in the dark,
I wonder at my eyes -
do they really see?

I feel blinded,
surrounded
by a wall of ice.

Muffling that which
sees so clearly -
the heart.

I wonder -
how long will I last -
lurking in the penumbra,
gazing longingly
at the sun,
but kept in the shadows.

For although I remain
hidden,
I take joy,
and some pleasure
at those
that revel
in the sun.

For I am envious
of their joy,
but in a bizarre way,
I gain pleasure -
something about
experiencing the joy
second handedly.

And as I watch,
I dream of the shadows
where I hide,
comforting
in their darkness.

A familiar companion
to a dark soul.

- title by KS

## 40. The Unseen - 2000.05.02

At so many strokes past
midnight,
I remember,
that I am,
the unseen.
I hear,
the unheard.
I remember,
the forgotten.

To live vicariously
through others.

I struggle to remember
myself -
if there is such a thing.

For I am
molded by expectations-
and must fulfill
them first.

As the words run across the
page,
I am reminded
of their permanence.

- title by KS

## 41. 2000.05.08

Angst
slowly
my heart freezes
and in the middle
I hear a gasp -
a clenching of the organ
against the choke around it.

And as my fingers slow
and my eyes slowly shutter,
I remember the bitter
sweet taste that filled
my mouth.

## 42. Harsh - 2000.05.05

Harsh intrusions on life
means that
my hand falls away
from the tablet it held.

## 43. Reminder - 2000.05.11

A subtle reminder to myself
of the emptiness that surrounds
us

Cushioned in the business
of the day
we are reminded of the hollow
nights.

A slow pain
tears through
the hours
calling to us
a fellow traveler
of the lonely road.

As it winds past
the white picket fence
on a path overgrown
with weeds.

The house is abandoned
a ruined effigy
of what once was.

Soon,
we move beyond the road,
searching for another path
that might take us
to the water.

So that my single boat
might take me
to the island
of my lonely days.

## 44. Storm Clouds - 2000.05.12

Quickly the lightning
moves across the sky
followed by the rumblings
of a far-off thunder.

And my heartbeat jumps
in time with the storm.

And so I return
to the barren landscape
that has captivated my attention
outshining all the others.

And as the storm clouds near,
I remember the gentle rains
of yesterday,
warm and wet weather...

- title by KS

## 45. Two - 2000.05.15

Two is the number
that is prime.

For the path that two hearts
travel
is such that we never see
the tears they shed
the laughter they share
and the joy
they find together.

It is always
more than twice the fun
and much less than twice the
sorrow

It is seldom
the time that we remember
spending it with
the other half
for
no longer is
one plus one
two
but one.

It is two hearts
sharing
one memory,
two souls
living
one day.

## 46. Three - 2000.05.15

Three is the number
for stability.
For there is no longer
a simple
you
and
I.
But we.

It becomes more than just
two lives apart
but one life together
and we are reminded
that both you
and I
carry memories
and together
we make more.

## 47. Infinity - 2000.05.16

There are no words
to describe
the depth of happiness
you inspire

I cannot begin
to express the feelings
that bubble through
every time
my thoughts
turn towards you

Everything that I see
carries a remembrance
of your smiling eyes
that I willingly
drown in

Every sound I hear
carries your voice
to my ears
your honeyed words
that both inflame
and sooth
at the same time

Every breath I take
reminds my heart
of the other
that laid so close

Every thought consumes me
in a slow heat
that captures my attention
more surely
than a thousand lights

Every step I take
is on the path
towards you,
seeking that day
when our lives
are more than just
the sum of our
phone calls,
and email
and fleeting days together

I look to that time
where our separation
is measured in minutes
and not weeks

Where our memories
outlast our loneliness

Where our life together
stretches past
our lives apart.

## 48. Rain - 2000.05.16

The droplets land quickly
against heated skin
leaving that brief sizzle
as the warmth
of my flesh catches the rain

I watch the storm clouds gather
darkening the sky
and I remember
that day
where you and I
spent a happy time
dancing
in the spring rains

Our happy innocence
was replaced by
soft touches and
an afternoon spent
in front
of the fire

And as I stand out here
in this brief storm
I travel back
to that day
where my memories
are so fresh

And I can only feel
the wet misery
that the rain leaves
and I slowly
return
to an emptiness
that echoes through
my heart

## 49. Hidden - 2000.05.17

Hidden in the shoals
of the mind
are the subtle horrors of
a life not lived,
of a half-made attempt
at finding strength

Hidden is the
tightening of the fist
surrounding the heart
squeezing in distress
and never forgetting
the pain
that drives us
slowly
towards a precipice
where we dangle
like puppets
at the hands of
our own fate

Hidden
are the pangs of guilt
that assail you
in the middle of the night
when comfort cannot
be sought nor
given

Hidden
is the pain
behind the brighter smile
and clearest laughter
like a grey cloud
behind the morning sun

Hidden are my memories
in the maze that is my mind

to be packed away
in a small black box
only to be seen
in that lightless place
where we reside

Hidden
is the cost of pain
that is tolled each time
I read this
knowing full well
that the pain
does not go away

A cost that we pay
each time we think,
each moment we feel

Hidden
is the melancholy
that rules me.

## 50. Demons - 2000.05.17

As I sit here
in the dark
a slow paralysis
overtakes me

And I forget that
I can feel
and slowly
my mind flees
from the demons of
my past
only to find them
in my future

And as I watch
the shadows fall
across the walls,
the darkness has
caught up with me

The comfort of the shadows
is nothing
compared to the
pain that runs strongly.

-title by KS

## 51. Shadows - 2000.05.16

I sit here
in the dusky shadows
as the moon wanes
and my mind
turns inside

Wandering down dark alleys
and hidden corners
I pick
at the memories that
are hidden here

Grey light is shed
across these dank corners
with solemn pain
that cannot be seen
in the light of day

My breath catches
as I come across
happy memories

For that is all they are -
a carefully hoarded
snapshot
of days gone by
when one was not a lonely
number
but a moment apart.

Cautiously I sift
through something
that was
but is no more

And a bittersweet pang
of pain arches across
nerves long raw

A certain wryness crosses
the mind
- at the deliberateness as
we pick at this scab
only to uncover
a pain
that has not
healed.

## 52. Storm - 2000.05.18

The steady rain
comes down
and
scintillates
as
it runs down
the window

My eyes are drawn
repeatedly
to the
hardy souls
outside

The coolness of the rain
dampens the dreams
of yesterday
when
today
held so much
promise.

## 53. Sunshine - 2000.05.18

As I basked in the bright
sunlight
I am drawn back to that day
where we spent
an afternoon outside
breathing in the crisp
spring air.

My memories are cast
in the golden light
of your smile.

Carefully,
I treasure each moment
and wrap it in the softest
of linens
and we relive each moment
in its time.

## 54. Life Line - 2000.05.18

Twisting
I grasp for the line
that keeps me
amongst the living.

Once more,
I am reminded
of the times where I
once knew who I was
and my place in the world.

But such securities
no longer exist
and I search for
these places again.

My eyes are tired
and unwillingly leave
the words that
would mean most.

-title by KS

## 55. Sunlight - 2000.05.20

In the shadowed world I thrive
and
dream of sunshined love;
like the hidden secrets of the
night
I shy away from the light

It is a constant dance -
I dream yet fear the light
disappearing with the rising sun
I wonder
if it matters
that sunlight is something
that I am seeking

Seeking, spurning
this cycle never ends
one day
I say,
one day,
I too, shall find something
that would hold
the shadows in the sunlight -
if nothing,
but to throw it in sharp relief.

## 56. 2000.05.20

As my eyes close
my mind is drawn to your image
and I dream
of the happier days
gone by.

Vivid colours are painted
across the barren lands.
006b. The Battle - 2000.05.20
Today,
the anger pours in steady waves
as I stand and watch
the words fly.

The fury builds as I watch
the hidden wounds open
and the subtle pain begin.

Your eyes betray your disgust
as I'm sure mine do
and I struggle to muffle
the bitterness
that must exude.

I wonder
is it valour that keeps me
from the rejoinder?

Or is it a recognition
of the futility
to argue against a wall.

And we turn away
with a betrayed face
as I hide once more.

Withdrawing from the
battlefield
is a matter of routine.

And my silence is not surrender
but a fact.

And my resolve is not to
answer your set ways
but to remind myself
of my own.

-title by KS

## 57. Afloat - 2000.05.20

The river flows steadily
pulsing at a constant rate
and I watch
in morbid fascination
as its red pearls
drip
slowly.

Each word I hear,
each minute I wait,
slowly
I
float
down river.

As it speeds up,
I look for
the shore.

-title by KS

## 58. "Wish you were here…"
– 2000.05.20

I watch
the sun rise
as the mist lay upon the leaves
and the hazy image
brings back
memories
that we shared.

Of warm glances
and hot kisses
under the palm fronds
where it didn't matter
that all we shared
were a few moments
of time.

Carefully, I memorize
the image
engraving it in my minds eye
where once more
I look back
to those days.

## 59. Searching – 2000.05.20

Searching
for that other piece
to fit life's puzzle.

I find
looking for love
in all the wrong places
to be
an adventure
of its own.

And each bend I turn
I see something new

And like an indolent cat
I am in no rush
to find that
piece
preferring to learn
as I go.

To ask as I need
and hope to find.

-title by KS

## 60. Dazed Memories - 2000.05.21

As I sat outside today,
I basked in the bright sunlight
and thought of you...
the happiness and warmth
that you brought.

I mused at the memories
of summer picnics
and shouts of laughter.

Spending the time
ogling all of those that passed
our way.

And like a cat,
I turned over to dream
of the more lazy days of summer.

Only to awaken and realize
that the sun has set
and a chill pervades me
as all I have left
are these few memories.

## 61. Volleys - 2000.05.21

It was like a soap opera
seeing the unthinkable;
the first time we meet
to be over a bed
with you silently within.

To be asked -
"you are?"
the first shot
an eyebrow raised.

"A friend"
is the return volley.

And so the game begins
switching from
Blind Man's Bluff
to charades.

## 62. Ice Cream - 2000.05.23

As I watch the cherry stems float
on the white vanilla river,
the chocolate silt is carried
along.

And slowly,
the strawberry barges nudge
closer to the glass bowl edge
where they are picked up
in a steel lift
and dropped into a dark
emptiness.
Only to hear the hums of
pleasure.

## 63. Reflections - 2000.05.21

The crisp cool weather
chills my skin
and dampens the soul
as I lay watching
the moon rising
and the few stars appear.

As I turn once more,
I catch a glimpse of your eyes
in the reflected window
and wonder at my sight
for it is impossible to have been
you.

And I ponder
on the reasons why -
chief amongst them -
our days apart
now outnumber the days
together
and certainly,
distance cannot bridge
two souls.

Slowly turning away
from the memories
of a happy time
where we needed no light
to brighten our days.

Once more
my eyes are drawn
to that
shadowed corner.

I blink.

And the shadow has
disappeared.


## 64. the Train - 2000.05.22

Like a train I run...
there are no stops
except for the beginning
and the end
and once there
I cannot stay
and so it goes.

To stop is to ask
for the sun to hide;
to look for hope where none
is to be found;
to want something
that is impossible;
and for such,
to desire
is improbable.

To dream -
a stray hope,
and to seek -
a mere thought.

-title by KS

## 65. Rhythmic Implosion - 2000.05.22

Each pulsation
adds to the tension
within
and the careful watch
continues.

And as each beat is sounded,
nerves are stretched taut.

And once the fray is run,
the implosion begins
each moment in time
building.

## 66. The Cutting Word - 2000.05.22

Each word is like a cut
and every time I read them
I relive the moment
that I wrote them.

Each day is like a wound -
open, raw
and unhealing.
And each time I write
I remember.

Every silent moment is hard won
for there is
no peace in constant struggle.

Each life is a vacuum -
unfeeling of the pain

for all my thoughts
have been recorded
and I am
empty
now.

-title by KS

## 67. Breakout - 2000.05.22

Grounded in reality
I see the thoughts take flight
and their freedom
brings a vague sense
of closure.

For even as I stand here
half-hidden by the shadows
I must remember
that some part
of my soul
is within the light
and strange hopes
of being remembered
may even be
realized
as I see my
lifetime
written out
in
words.

-title by KS

## 68. The Puzzle - 2000.05.22

The subtle heat
causes the land to shimmer
as I wait
for the time to pass.

And I watch
the crowds pass by
looking for that puzzle piece
to finish the picture
I build.

In fact,
all I may be missing
are the eyes
for they carry a sparkle
unmatched by the stars
and when they twinkle,
I shiver with anticipation
and when they glimmer
with tears
I can only hope that
it is from happiness
and not sorrow.

-title by KS

## 69. Dreams Aloft - 2000.05.22

The flock of birds
took flight
and I sent my dreams
with them.

And as I watched their southern
path,
I gave my hopes free reign
sending them as well...

I hope there comes a day
where my thoughts and body
will be joined
and I would travel
amongst the flocks...

-title by KS

## 70. Envy - 2000.05.22

The pounding of the waves
echoes the beating of my heart
and I watched
the cries of the gulls
with hidden envy.

The summer breeze soothes me
and I dream
of the butterflies
that gather
amongst the field flowers.

No longer are my thoughts
for spring fancy
but turn to finding
something that lasts
beyond the summer nights.

-title by KS

## 71. Images - 2000.05.22

Upon a crisp clean page
these words fall
carefully carving
an image from
a shapeless form
with chosen precision.

I realize
that I paint an indelible picture
upon my mind.

And each day that passes,
I store away
the images
that strike me.

-title by KS


## 72. Full Steam Ahead - 2000.05.22

Like a train
I am running
at full speed
on this simple line
away from that which ails me
into the
unforgiving wilderness
where survival
is by the fittest.

There are no stops
on this one-way line
no conductor
nor director either
and like an
automaton
we proceed.

-title by KS


## 73. Questions - 2000.05.22

How do you explain
togetherness
to someone who's always been
apart?

How do you explain heartbreak
to someone who's never been
alone?

How do you explain happiness
to someone who has nothing to
compare?

How do you say "I love you"
when you've never heard it
yourself?

## 74. The Darkness Within - 2000.05.23

As the night sets in
my mind turns over
to delve into
the darkness within
that surely outweighs
that without.

And I wonder
what spurs me to do this?
To willing let go
of bits of myself
when I can't
even bear to think of them.

Like old scabs
I pick at these thoughts
until the wave of
icy coldness floods down
and engulfs all that I do.

-title by KS

## 75. Adrift - 2000.05.23

The rain
echoes outside
and already I feel sleepy
and carefully
I drift
and dream
of the sun,
of the laughter
that is so prevalent
outside.

As I float
on this haze
I wonder
if I can wait
for the days
to pass.

Or will my excitement
overwhelm me?

-title by KS

## 76. Rain - 2000.05.23

As I watch the speckling
of rain drops against the window
I look past the blurry images
and imagine that
tomorrow will bring back
the sunshine
that warms my life.

And I watch
the shimmering lights
reflect off the puddles
and laugh
at the sudden urge
to stomp outside
amongst the
gasoline rainbows.

-title by KS

## 77. Words of Hate - 2000.05.23

I wonder
what would happen
if the world
suddenly came to a stop
and if the words
of hate
were expunged?

Would there be more love
and less hate?
More peace
and less war?

Would we put more effort
into understanding another
in place
of explaining yourself?

-title by KS

## 78. Others - 2000.05.23

Like the fly that dreams of the spider,
I wonder at the fascination
that we carry
for the forbidden
for the "others"
that are so ostracized.

Is it some type of "perverse"
shame
that one hears of?
- the constant harping
of the differences
that lie between
"us"
and
"them."

Who is "us" and who are "they"?
Why do we fixate
on their "oddities"
instead of looking for
the similarities?

Why are we searching
for reasons
to exclude,
instead of all the ways
that we have to include?

-title by KS

## 79. Shelter of a Smile - 2000.05.24

I dream
of the life
beyond four walls
as I reach
for the doors
that open to
a time afar
from this.

When I can look back
to the life as it was -
a period of
existence
as opposed to
true living.

I remember when
my struggles overwhelmed
my thoughts
and the only shelter
given
is a simple
smile.

-title by KS

## 80. Remembering - 2000.05.24

As I watch you smile
I look back
at all the warmth
I've seen

And I choose this moment
to memorize your grin
that carries that slight
twinkle in your eyes -
and the quirk of your lips.

Like a crisp June night
where I counted the
arrival of the evening stars;
each time you smile,
differs.

-title by KS

## 81. Counting - 2000.05.26

They say that one must die
a thousand deaths
to live a life.

And so I count;
I have died a thousand days
for every hour
that I lived.

And I have learnt
to treasure every memory
as the days pass
for time is fleeting
and loss
unexpected.

And the words run
like drops on a page
dripping red and black
against white
only to blur at the end.

-title by KS

## 82. Outside - 2000.05.27

The warm sun outside
beckons to me
and I look outside
to watch
the verdant fields
slightly sway
in the gentle wind.

As the pale green leaves
drift
I watch
them float
on the breeze
and imagine
myself
outside.

-title by KS

## 83. Visiting - 2000.05.27

As I watch
the landmarks
whisk by
I am reminded
that it has
been too long
since I have visited.

As much as I know the land,
it looks different
when I am just
the passenger.

Always, my eyes
look outward -
past crisp leaves
and bright flowers.

To watch the small
flocks of sparrows
and robins cheer.

-title by KS

## 84. Deafening - 2000.05.27

The din is deafening
and my head aches
with the thunder that
echoes within.

Hearing but not understanding
the feeling reverberates
through my bones

As I wait
for the earthquakes
to roll through.

-title by KS

## 85. Fudge Brownie Cheesecake... - 2000.05.27

The slow dribble
drips carefully
and we are watching
in near-captive
fascination.

In a pool of white,
the dark chocolate lies
in swirls and shimmering
lights.

As you slice away at
the mound of white,
it slowly melts
along the edge...

The slow descent
of light ice cream
and dark chocolate
draws our attention
away from that
intensely red cherry
that lay nestled
in the cradle
of white cream.

A short lick
and a white moustache
is all that is left.

... to LLJS, who traveled a
thousand miles and for whom I
write this pome.

## 86. I Wonder - 2000.05.28

I wonder what would happen
if she realized
that I heard
but never understood,
never acknowledged,
and proceed on my course.

Would there be anger?
Frustration?
Exasperation?
Hate?

I wonder
if I would
feel anything
more than the
emptiness
within.

Where a crisp north wind
blows across
the barren lands.

I wonder
if my indifference
would aggravate you more
if you knew it?

And so I remain
silent
in your diatribe.

And I dream
of the emptiness.

-title by KS

## 87. Islands - 2000.05.28

In a sea of humanity
we are lonely islands
where the waves
of emotion
wash along the shore.

Through the ages
the archipelagoes
rise from
the ocean floor -
connected by circumstance
and birth
but apart yet the same.

And even though
fisherman may
occasionally stop,
none make their home
on the island,
for both distance
and irrelevance
separate it from the others.

-title by KS

## 88. Untitled - 2000.05.28

As the clouds shift
my gaze wanders
to those that are around me
and I am
captured in their snippets
of life that I see.

I imagine
that their lives are just
as complex
as a Gordian knot.

## 89. Untitled - 2000.05.28

The crisp breeze
blows across the lake
and the joggers
pace on the boardwalk.

## 90. The Number Question - 2000.05.28

Zero
is an oddly even
beginning
and end.

For naught
has been exchanged -
there is only
nothingness
that
I return to.

And such is zero
that its outside
is framed
but its inside
is empty.

Though a number,
its usefulness lies
in its neutrality -
for any movement
on its part
changes its being.

## 91. "Questions" - 2000.05.28

You asked,
"have you ever?"
and I said, "no."

And we stopped.

The you asked,
"are you looking?"
and I said, "no."

And I wondered
how many more times
would I respond "no"
to something,
that for others,
would have been
a different answer.

## 92. Untitled - 2000.05.29

These words cut
deeper than the
roughest blade.

Carving slow pieces
of flesh -
a pound
for each thought.

And so they lie
like so much rubbish -
skin shed
like a snake.

Dried, shapeless
in a harsh sun.

They bake and harden
in the light
shriveling
into
nothingness.

## 93. Deathwatch - 2000.05.29

1 2 3 4
slowly counting
the days that I live
the ways that I died.

For every year of existence
I have lived but half a day
and those are far and long apart.

Stolen moments
in a year of emptiness
I awaken only
to realize
that it has passed.

And the return to
somnolence has begun,
as the cloak descends
unfeelingness
and distance
swirl
sheltering the memories
from sunlight.

- title by TC

## 94. Wonderful Twos - 2000.05.29

I have captured
a lifetime in two days;
I have lived
in laughter for two hours;
I have gathered my soul
for two moments.

And like two halves,
the rotation has changed
to finding
two moments of peace
in twenty years of strife;
of finding
two words of love
in twenty lives of hate,
of hoping
for two tears of happiness
in twenty ages of sorrow.

And I am disappointed
only by myself;
for seeking the impossible,
for daring to dream
amongst nightmares.

-title by KS

## 95. Untitled - 2000.05.29

When I look,
I see nothing
worth keeping,
worth mourning,
worth crying for

When I search,
I find nothing
less desired,
less kept,
less wanted.

When I hear,
I find silence,
no thought,
no emotion,
no smile.

When I feel,
I find pain,
I find shadows,
I find sharpness.

And so the reflection shatters
like a thousand
slivers of glass
and my eyes close
once more.

## 96. Black Box - 2000.05.29

In the shadows I hide,
like a box
in a forgotten home.

Having seen sunlight once,
I retreat to the comfort
of darkness.

Where everything is muted
and welcoming
to our own dark secrets.

And every time I lurk,
I gather the darkness
around me,
absorbing all the words
that slice surer
than a surgeons' blade.

And so the words pour
from the box
onto the page,
so many droplets seen
crimson in their freshness.

-half of the title by KS

## 97. Untitled - 2000.05.29

I live at night
to die a day
and always I remember

To thank the night
for letting death
pass me unfettered

And each day I struggle
to live once more
in the darkness
that surrounds us.

## 98. Withdrawing - 2000.05.30

In a shroud of darkness
I lumber
like a mockery to grace
and
under the cover of no stars
I appear
like the remnants of a flood
unwanted
and unneeded.

And like the tides
I recede
into the shallows,
trapped
in a pool of water

And slowly
I withdraw
until
all that is left,
are faint rings of salt.

-title by KS

## 99. Sunset - 2000.05.30

In a brilliant sky of
deep purples and dark reds
the sun sets
like a red monster
on the evening sky.

And gradually,
the wisps of clouds
move away from
the horizon -
white streaks
on a dark sky.

As the night darkens
I watch the twinkling
of city lights
begin
perched on the top
of a point
where we watched
the busyness of the day
become the nightlife.

-title by KS

## 100. The Dance - 2000.05.30

Amongst sharp shadows
and soft murmurs
the couples dance
weaving through
the moonlight.

And their careful dips
and curtseys
mirrored after life
give grace to
a trial of wills -
where one leads
and the other one follows
only to smoothly switch
on the next turn.

-title by KS

## 101. Untitled - 2000.05.31

120 pages
like 50 ways to leave your lover
holds the thoughts
in tidy order.

Each page is like a beacon
carrying some thought to shore.

Setting some adrift,
each time is slightly different -
no two thoughts alike -
no two times the same.

And like a dream,
struggling to capture the
thoughts,
I reach for pen
and paper once more.

## 102. Misfit - 2000.05.31

Like a white-bread girl
in a whole wheat world
I fit,
but only slightly.

And look for something
that masquerades as love.

In desperate haste,
I ponder
how much of this
is worth fighting for?

This elaborate dance
amongst two
is an exchange
of soft glances
and warm touches.

Sharing between two
what cannot be found
by one.

-title by KS

## 103. Have you ever... 2000.06.01

Have you ever
sat up a whole night
because your thoughts
would not stop?

Have you ever
thought of the darkness
as your friend
because it sheltered you
from eyes?

Have you ever
run away
because it was
more painful to stay?

Have you ever
dreamt of heaven
knowing that you
lived in hell?

Have you ever
sought to deafen
the silence,
so that you
could sleep?

Have you ever
thought to blind
yourself,
so that you would
not have to see?

Have you ever
fallen into a hole
only to be told
that it was your grave?

Have you ever
thought of living
as something beyond
surviving?

Have you ever
sought to dream,
if only to escape
your nightmares?

## 104. Captured Images - 2000.06.02

I dream in black and white
of things that happen
in living color.

And like moving pictures
I capture them
only
once
with words
that struggle
to describe
their beauty.

And like a fickle heart,
the thoughts escape me
but manage to
flow onto
the page of white.

-title by KS

## 105. The Patient Lover - 2000.06.02

I catch the silver
moonbeams in my palm,
at awe of the
bright light

And I dream
of bright nights
and sweet songs
if for no other
reason
than, I can.

And like a patient lover,
I pour all my thoughts
to her
knowing that the moon
will safely guard them.

And so,
I spend hours
turning watchful gaze
to her splendour.

-title by KS

## 106. Light - 2000.06.03

Faster than light travels
do my dreams
and thoughts
imprint themselves
in the arms of another.
And like the depths of heavenly
darkness,
do I willingly
let myself
fall into that state
of happiness
knowing that I float amongst
the highest of clouds on
pure love and contentment.

Every effort to clearly describe
the emotions I feel
are thwarted
by
the words
that limit
every nuance.

And like an exploding star
I bask in the light
that cascades
around me.

## 107. 2000.06.03

The gentle winds of spring
are a soft caress
against bare arms.

The bright sun
is a warm smile
against my eyes.

The warmth that
surrounds me
does not even begin
to match
the sense of
satisfaction
that overwhelms me.

## 108. 2000.06.04

Many years from now,
I shall walk again
across this sandy beach.

And hear the sighing of the trees
as they rustle in the wind
to brush against my hand.

I shall feel again
the power of the waves
battling against the sand,
to marvel at the quiet strength
of nature in the wild autumn
winds.

Someday when I am tired,
I will want to remember
my days with the beach.

Wanting to retrace
steps impressed upon
the shifting sands
of so many years ago.

## 109. 2000.06.04

Every time
the sun rises
so do my dreams disperse
and like the wisps of clouds
do they appear
every so often.

And my eyes turn
to the bright sunlight
and I am reminded
that the only sight
more beautiful
would be the
happiness
in her eyes.

And the only sight clearer
than a summer sky
would be the smile
on her lips.

## 110. Love - 2000.06.04

Across the distance
two souls meet
and realize
that neither age,
distance
nor time
could separate
something
that so filled
their hearts.

So in an age
where "love" is just a word
bandied
about,
it's always a pleasure
to see that
love flourishes
still.

-title by KS

## 111. 2000.06.05

If two hearts loved
would anyone else need to
know?
For what is shared
to be between just two
and not a thousand?

If two lives parted
would they shatter
into a thousand pieces -
and be beyond repair?

If two hearts fought
would they love enough
to say
"I'm sorry"
and hear in return
"you're forgiven."?

If two hearts
felt
the same
would they still
remain separate?

## 112. Candles Light - 2000.06.07

In the wee hours of the morning
I dream
of turning over
to see your bright eyes

In the earliest part of the day
I wonder
about these lonely nights

Where we treasure
every moment together
and hunger from
every moment apart

And like a candles light
I reach out in the darkness
for your shadow.

-title by KS

## 113. At Sea - 2000.06.08

A sudden coldness grasps me
and the pain twists inside
so that breathing is
now an option
as opposed
to being
a necessity.

And like a cool stiletto
the words carve a neat line
through the fog.

And carefully
I pour the words,
the thoughts,
onto a white page.

And watch them sail
like so much flotsam
into the sea
- where it struggles
to stay afloat
only
to sink
once more.

-title by KS

## 114. The Difference - 2000.06.08

The difference between living
and just existing
is feeling.

To live
you must feel
everything,
every nuance,
every pain,
and like a boat,
go with the waves
or sink.

To exist,
you do not feel
and just work,
eat,
sleep,
with nothing that
excites you,
disturbs you,
or even bothers you.

- This pome is for KS - who
reminded me that the stanza:
"Have you ever thought of living
as something beyond surviving."
was good.

- Title by KS *g*

## 115. Slide Rule - 2000.06.09

On a sliding scale
where do love and like
separate?

On the road to life,
when do you know
you've reached love?

How do we know
that we're not
settling for "like"
when we want "love"?

- title by KS


## 116. If You Knew - 2000.06.09

If you knew what lay beneath,
would you still ask?

If you knew how much it hurt,
would you still want?

If you know how dark it was,
would you still read?

-title by KS


## 117. Hidden Treasures - 2000.06.10

The white sun
on burnished flesh
brings out the
brightness of your smile.

And I listen for the laughter
that follows,
as the slow drip
of the ice cream
against your fingers
makes for a mess
that is a joy to clean,
as I watch
the pink tip
of your tongue
carefully lick
every crevice
where the ice cream hides.

And reluctantly,
my eyes draw upward
to see the slight grin
on your lips.

- Title suggested by TC

**118.** On summer days,
thoughts turn to... - 2000.06.10

On a hot summers day,
the ice cream looks
especially inviting
against the pale surface
of your skin

And my eyes follow
the pattern
of the cool cream,
spackled against your lips,
knowing that slow nibbles
become hot kisses
as it melts.

My anxiousness to
clean the surface
leaves it glistening
as I listen to your
short breaths
heavy against my ears.

With a deliberate hand,
I raise another spoonful -
missing your mouth
as the white drops fall,
landing on your throat.

With mumbled apologies,
I watch the writhing
as the mixture
of cold dessert
and hot skin
creates a brief sizzle

And at that moment,
I want nothing more
than to be

the white ice cream
that has resettled itself
on your heated body.

Turning the cold spoon
against sensitive flesh,
there is a subtle tightening
as contact is made.

All across the expanse
of bare skin,
is the ice cream
and honey trailed -
your body serving as
the surface to partake of.

The sweetly sticky sensation
captivates the senses
as light nips
cause a slow dance
between flesh
and mouth -
your muffled demands
mixing with hums of pleasure.

- title courtesy of KS, MW, and Lurker #1

## 119. Wine - 2000.06.10

In the shimmering summer heat
the images are in a haze.
I watch
as the slivers of ice
melt against
your skin.

Playfully,
I drop the cool
shavings against your mouth
just to hear
your shrieks of protest
amongst the laughter.

Fascinated,
I watch the rich burgundy wine
against the clear glass
as a steady pulse beats
at the hollow of your throat.

And succumbing to temptation,
a mouthful of wine
finds itself
poured past your lips
to flow down the line
of your neck.

And like a wanderer
in the desert,
my eyes
follow its path,
only to be
edged out by sweet kisses.

## 120. Sounds - 2000.06.11

The moonlight casts a pale sheen
on all that lays under.

And the muted sounds
of life beyond
filters through
the window.

It is an emptiness echoed
from within
that thunders through the mind.

And like all sounds...
it fades away...

-title by KS

## 121. What... - 2000.06.12

What price is paid for peace,
when outer serenity masks
the inner turmoil?

What life is lived by half
when it is not your own?

What time is free to use
when it is filled by others?

What voice is heard aloud
when it is silenced from within?

What thoughts are kept apart
when they are all too crowded?

- title suggestions from KS, MW,
and L#1

## 122. Endless Trial - 2000.06.13

In a haze of confusion
I am searching
for answers
to questions unasked

And so I wonder,
how fair it is to those
around me
to have to share
the contradictions I find

For every answer I think found,
I ask another,
and like a Mobius strip
it is a continuous journey
of questions and answers

On an endless trial
to self-knowledge,
a meandering path is drawn
with no beginning
and no real end.

-title by KS

## 123. In the middle of the night... - 2000.06.13

In the middle of the night,
there is always one moment
where darkness and light
struggle for dominance.

And as the shadows recede,
the moon wanes
and time marches on.

A careful eye
notes the shifting
of the tides
to reveal
a solemn figure
half hidden in
the shadows.

- title suggested by KS, S, and K

## 124. Trap of Fear - 2000.06.14

When you walk down the roads,
and see the path before you...
do you wonder,
why the sharp words hurt more
than the stones...
why you're lost
even if the path is straight?
why you're in a daze
even if everyone else is lucid?

When you dream aloud,
do you mention the time spent,
the people,
and the laughter?

Or do you shy away from it all...
caught in a trap of fear?

-title by KS

## 125. Something for Tomorrow - 2000.06.15

In a time
where we are concerned with
now, here,
and the urgency of today...

How often do we think about
tomorrow?
How often do we put aside
something
for tomorrow?

When we have more time
more energy
more strength
to do
to see
to hear...

Only to realize
that when now is "later" -
we no longer have
the stamina,
the vision
or the time
to do all
that we hoped for.

-title by KS

## 126. Love Is - 2000.06.15

Like a snowflake
love is.

Like the colours of
the spectrum
blending hues
and intensities

No two times
the same,
no two lives
more different.

And on the palette
we mix two lives
and create
a new colour -
brighter in color,
stronger in life.

It becomes a careful
addition
to the colorful
woven web.

-title by KS

## 127. A Pale Reflection - 2000.06.15

There are no words
to capture
the emotions
and things
I see.

And like
a blind man's
effort
to describe
the rising sun,
these words
are
a
pale
reflection
of
the
truth.

-title by KS

## 128. Inside Out - 2000.06.16

From the outside,
we look in,
to see two lives
entwined together.

From the inside,
they look out,
at the world
that surrounds them.

And as the threads unwind,
to drift apart once more,
two hearts break
from inside out.

## 129. Lassitude - 2000.06.17

In bright sunlight
and warm summer air
there is a lassitude
around us
that makes for
slow afternoons

And I watch
the clouds move
across the crisp blue sky.

Dreaming of hot days
and cool nights
where
a warm breeze
is all that moves.

- title suggested by S

## 130. Train Station - 2000.06.18

Everything I feel,
see and hear,
is sublimated
into my writing.

All the questions I ask,
all the confusion I see -
form part of the thoughts
laid out.

-title by KS

## 131. Hollow - 2000.06.19

Hollow is the feeling
when no one wins,
and everyone losses.

Limping, battered
off the rough field,
two hearts
are wounded once more.

Painful is the news
to the surroundings
where we are.

Saddened am I
at the end of a time
where happiness and joy
were the feelings
of the day.

-title by KS

## 132. Summer Games - 2000.06.19

In the late summer afternoon
sun
I watched the ice
melt
off
your tongue
just in time
for me to catch
the last droplet.

Hot warmth
and cold shivers
are a
delightful
contrast
on your skin.

-title by KS

## 133. Moonbeams - 2000.06.20

In the bright moonlight
everything takes on
an ethereal glow
casting hazy shadows
on hidden corners.

And like a single moonbeam
my thoughts turn outwards
to record the happiness
of two -
having found
something important,
an intangible gift.

- title by KS

## 134. Captive - 2000.06.20

The eyes are the first clue
at the utter captivity
that we are held -
drowning
in the pools of green

And like star-struck gawkers,
we hesitate to draw breath
as the sparkle of your eyes
peek out at us.

- title by KS

## 135. Strange Love - 2000.06.20

In a time where every time is now,
love takes on the meaning of forever.

In a life where everything is here,
love takes on the place of "there."

In an age where everyone is
alone,
love means "together."

///

Why do we choose to run away,
when we should move towards?

Why do we choose to hide,
when we have found?

Why do we question
when we should just accept?

-title by KS

## 136. Malibu - 2000.06.21

Like a dot,
my eyes follow
the curving shoreline
that hugs the
cliff side.

A crisp sea spray
mists on the road
as the smooth ride
continues.

Weaving through the
speckled sunlight,
slight breeze in your hair,
your laughter
blends with the air.

## 137. Summer Solstice - 2000.06.21

On the longest day of the year,
I watch the waning of the stars
as the night air creeps in
to whisper
the secrets
of the world
into my ears.

And like a conch shell,
I hear the songs
of the world
in my mind.

## 138. Leather and Silk - 2000.06.21

Slipping and sliding
the water droplet
falls down
the line of your back
as I look upwards
to drown
in
your smile.

And like supple curves
on the silk,
there is a certain comfort
in the cool warmth
that you wear.

Like the caress of the sunlight
against tendrils of gold
there is a brilliant shine
that is reflected
in your eyes.

As I watch
the slick glide
of leather
against silk,
I find myself
envious
of the close contact
of chilled cloth
on heated flesh.

-title by KS

## 139. Mischief - 2000.06.21

The salty sweat drips
and a slow lick
crosses your lips
as a slight smile
emerges.

Fingers trace the path
that my eyes
carve against
the slick surface.

A low chuckle
floats to my ears
and brings a
wicked sparkle
to your eyes.

As my fingers wander,
short breaths
and silent gasps
are music
to my ears.

- title by KS

## 140. Helpless - 2000.06.22

The heart breaks
from the inside
as I watch
from afar

Helpless to do anything
but wanting to do so much

And each time
we meet,
the pain is renewed -
have you seen her?

It serves as a bitter reminder
of the frailty of love -
where doubt and worries
are the heaviest burden

Where the want of courage
means the end
of a flowering light.

- title by KS

## 141. Confusion - 2000.06.23

The thoughts in my head
run amuck
like pinball's after break.

And confusion descends
like a familiar miasma,
enshrouding me once more.

And my tired eyes
can barely focus,
never mind see
the dancing figures in front.

-title by KS

## 142. Sunrise - 2000.06.24

The sunrise
was beautiful this morning.

Within the grey horizon
a lightening of the sky -
a pale pink, then yellow
against grey-blue.

The shadowed world of
early morning,
brought into sharp contrast
as the sun rose.

## 143. Dykes on Bikes - 2000.06.24

The roar of engines
drowned the cheers
from the crowds
and the gleam and shine
of the motor beasts
reflect the bright sunlight.

Flags of colour
flutter in the air
vibrating motors,
shiny leather,
caught up in the excitement
of the day.

Slick sweat,
sleek skin,
we watch
as the bikes
and the women that ride them
travel down the street -
followed by
happy shouts of laughter.

-title by KS

## 144. Peach - 2000.06.24

It was a sweetly
succulent peach
halved
that I first saw -
juices dripping
down your lips
gathering at your chin
as the nectar
on your lips
darken
to a deep sultry red
as your tongue
traced your mouth
once more.

## 145. Storm Clouds - 2000.06.24

The sky darkens
for the storm
as clouds gather
ominously above the land.

Heavy drops
splatter against
the window
where we sit
looking outside.

-title by KS

## 146. Waiting - 2000.06.25

Hot hazy humid days
make for late mornings
and languid afternoons.

We watch the storm clouds
gather
across the clear blue sky.

Eagerly we await the arrival
of crisp cool rain drops.

-title by KS

## 147. Contrasts - 2000.06.25

Outside, it was 100 degrees,
inside, just 68.

Outside, you were all warmth
and heat,
inside, you were frozen solid.

Outside, you grinned and
laughed,
inside, I never saw your smile.

Outside, I felt no warmth,
inside, I wonder what would stir
you.

-title by KS

## 148. Tears - 2000.06.26

The raindrops on the window
remind me of your tears -
sliding slowly
down your side.

And the image blurs
as the drops run together.

-title by KS

## 149. Filters - 2000.06.27

Living life in color,
I dream in black and white
and the filters
leach all the color,
draining vibrancy
to just memories.

And I wonder
at the vivacity
that is lost.

- title by KS

## 150. The Room - 2000.06.29

Emptiness
echoes through the room
where the dust motes
dance a lazy jig.

Hollow are the feelings
that remain -
a lifetime
of living
stored in these boxes

Shattered lives,
silent tears,
the shadows hold
many secrets

As the door closes
for one last time,
the room breathes
then shudders
once more.

- The attic - MW
- Storm Cellar - TC
- The Space - DM

151. Unchained - 2000.06.30

Like a chain
these words wind,
sinuous and long.

Catching the emotions
in a web of words.

And with a sudden twist,
the anguish presents itself
in a neat package
of a few lines.

- title by TC

152. When the Heart Breaks - 2000.06.30

In a sea of 20,000
when a heart breaks
is there anyone that hears this?

In a lifetime of millions,
how do two souls meet?

Thousands of times,
meeting and parting,
what value can be given
to something
that is a gift?

-title by KS

153. Summer Feast – 2000.06.30

Peaches halved
were sweetly glistening
under a clear liquid glaze

Bananas in clever slivers -
pale flesh against dark orange

Mangos' succulent flesh
nestled in between
the two halves

Two delectable mounds
of frozen white -
at crossways with
the peaches -
a pool of sweetness
gathers

Stiffened peaks
of white
are ladled on,
gently sliding off the tip
to land on
two sides of pale yellow
and dark gold

A sprinkling of chocolate
is spread across one peak
circling
the edge of the mound

Eyes light up
in delight
and then
laughter
as the golden strands
of butterscotch
twist
ever downwards.

- title by MW

## 154. Go for It - 2000.07.01

It was like watching
a dance -
gracefully athletic -
arms stretched out
as the ball floats
just out of reach
of the open hands.

A collective groan emerges
as a line is crossed
and bodies collide
in confusion.

-title by KS

## 155. Retreat - 2000.07.01

The bright sunlight
is followed by
a warm night breeze
as the sounds of darkness
echo outside.

The shadowy corners
beckon as I move
back inside
looking for
cooler climes.

- title by RF

## 156. Red Light - 2000.07.01

As cool clothes slide
against warm skin,
my eyes are drawn
ever upwards
as I begin to drift,
only to be brought back
to alertness as I watch
the pink tip
slide against
red lips.

- title by MW

## 157. Muse - 2000.07.02

For that she is my muse -
a silver body
and golden laughter.

Her two eyes
sparkle bright blue
in the sunlight,
four limbs
hugging tightly.

For where ever I go,
she follows,
carrying me safely
through time and distance.

## 158. Past Love Treasured - 2000.07.03

I saw the first bloom,
brilliant in color
foiled by the crisp green leaves
of new growth.

And as the days passed,
the flower grew
and opened up to
the sunshine
that was new love.

And as time passed,
it began to fade -
as the sun
did not reach the shade
where it lay
languishing.

Until finally,
this first rose
of the season
is to be pressed
in a page -
as the fragile
reminder of
first love.

- title suggestions by DM, TC, MW, and EM

## 159. Summer's Siesta - 2000.07.03

The red veil falls
over the golden sun
as the blue sky takes on
a deep magenta hue.

Against the brilliant dusk,
I watch as the flocks of birds
begin their yearly flight
in search of warmer climes.

Already, I am reminded
by the cooling evening breeze
that the short summer
is nearing end
and I too,
must prepare
for the return to
a stasis pattern
as all of nature's life
begins to fade.

- title suggested by TC

## 160. Collision of the Heart - 2000.07.04

Watching
in exaggerated motion
the collision
that would happen
I wondered at the
irreversibility
that seemed inherent.

And whether I could have,
somehow, prevented
this tragedy from occurring.

And like the horrific
image that it was,
my mind
persisted in replaying
every second
as I watched
the train
collide
into the sea.

- title suggestions by TC and KS

## 161. Drained - 2000.07.04

It was on that day
that I realized
that the cold floor
on which I lay
drained the warmth
from my bones,
as surely as
the words did
drain from my soul
and I came to know
that I was losing
much faster
than the knowledge
I gained.

Each word
was a part set free,
each note
was a feeling captured.

Until I lay -
hollow and empty
of all thoughts.

-title by KS

## 162. Vicarious - 2000.07.04

It was
a peripheral joy
that I took -
never quite mine
but the sharing of others.

It was
sustenance to a body
long starved
of emotion.

A husk of frail skin
and shattered bones.

-title by KS

## 163. Untitled - 2000.07.05

As I watch the signs
for a change in position
I am left with
the trepidation of waiting
to realize whether or not
I have moved beyond
self-sufficient
to independence.

And I wonder if
the year will pass
fast enough
so that I can set flight
my own dreams
travelling westwards
to the mountains.

And so it is:
my soul to the mountains
my life to the seas -
scattered as ashes
and floating.

## 164. Untitled - 2000.07.05

Was it exuberance
that I said yes to?
Was it reality
that I surrendered to?

To travel three thousand miles
for three days
I have but ten months
to cut strings,
build bridges
and find the lost
amongst the living.

## 165. Melting - 2000.07.06

What begins as the faintest drop
of white cream
on dark chocolate
rapidly expands
as the mound
of white grows
upwards.

Faintly decorated
by red cherries,
it is a vivid
contrast to the
pale orange of
the peach halves
that lay under.

As the cherry slips
down the white hill,
the pool spreads
outwards -
liquid white
on chocolate brown.

A path is carved
across light
and dark
as cuts are made
through the silent dessert.

All I can hear
are the sounds of
subtle savouring
of the cool treat.

- title suggestions by EFM, DM,
EM, RF and KS

## 166. Seduction - 2000.07.06

Thick golden strands
of liquid sunshine
slowly twine
into a hot pool -
moving first
to one side
and then to another
as the swirling pool
swallows the honey
in rapid descent.

This subtle dance
of seduction
continues as
a finger and then
a tongue
combine to lick
the last sweet
remnants
of honey
away from
the edge.

- title suggestions by KS, DM

## 167. Slumbers' Awakening - 2000.07.07

In the deepest hours
of the night
you can hear
the Earth breath
as we sleep
perchance to dream.

And as the balance
shifts from night to day,
we can hear no longer
as the receding shadows
take with them
our awareness
of all life.

Awakening - TC
Slumber - MW

## 168. Angel - 2000.07.07

An angel
in black and white
bent under
the weight
of the world.

And like Atlas' shoulders,
head ducked down,
finding all the hope
in a single rose.

The severe look
is softened only
by the slightest smile
on her lips.

## 169. Oreo Cookies - 2000.07.07

Round careful centers
of white
surrounded by dark layers
and I watched
the swirling
of the edge
against your tongue -
smoothing white cream
against dark chocolate.

Slowly twisting
one way
then another
as the separation
occurs,
there is a slight
pause
to watch
light and dark
part ways
once more.

## 170. A Trace of a Touch - 2000.07.08

In my mind's eye
I saw
the etched swirling
of dark
against pale
on an undulating
surface

And I reached out
with a phantom finger
to trace
the patterns
that you drew

Only to wish
for an endless journey
like a mobius strip
continually tracing
and finding new places
that I had not seen
before.

With the faintest
of touches,
following the curves
that ran in some
endless pattern,
I watched
the writhing
work its way
across the plains
of your skin.

-title by KS

## 171. Snapshots - 2000.07.08

Like a dream
where reality fades
to become the low hum
in the background,
attention focused
on only one -
vivid heat
and tepid cool
echoed strongly

Watching
the busyness
we live in
my eyes are caught
in an overflow
of images
cascading through
the words

Quickly the ink runs
catching the
faint ideas.

- title by KS

## 172. Untitled - 2000.07.08

As the noon sun overhead
shortened all the shadows
I am reminded
of the unending heat
that travels across the land
and fades
at the wall of ice.

## 173. Euphoria - 2000.07.08

The internal euphoria
is bubbling over,
pushing against
the pragmatism
that you see

Onwards
onwards
three hundred days of
euphoria,
angst
and worry

The price to be paid
for ten days
is more than worth
the thirty times
I must pay.

- title by KS

## 174. Sniper - 2000.07.09

It begins
like sniper fire
in a narrow alley -
every shot counts
every hit hurts.

Practice
and deliberate ignorance
are the only shields
against the
obvious barbs.

Watching the words,
prying them apart,
knowing their intent,
I have become inured
to them,
absorbing them,
mourning them,
shedding no tears for them.

I am not feeling them,
nor the excitement,
until I leave -
then I can feel.

## 175. Cocoon - 2000.07.09

I will be
moving into an
automatic state
of existence
where nothing will perturb me,
nothing will unhinge me,
where feeling is all
inside
only to seep out
onto the page.

This price I pay
for serenity
will not be high enough
if I can find some means
of happiness at the end.

I have three seasons to watch.

I have time to prepare
as I begin
to withdraw
to within.

- title by KS

## 176. Untitled - 2000.07.09

The silent screams echo
against the broken doorway
where I watch
voiceless lips
mouth
senseless words.

Amid the colorless landscape
of black and white,
I look for golden hopes
and silver linings -
knowing them to be
my disappointment.


## 177. Dawn - 2000.07.11

The early summer mornings
are cooled by a crisp breeze
that drifts within

And like the emerging sun
outside
the smile that creeps across
your lips
is just as gradual

The soft hum outside
is heard within
as the stillness
of the day's beginning
is broken
by a flurry of motion.

- title by KS


## 178. Raw - 2000.07.12

Raw
are the emotions you evoke;
like a summer storm
only the briefest notice
is given
as you decide
that the surprise
would be yourself.

Raw
is how I feel
as exposed as the
new sunrise
as you tug on
the hearts' strings.

-original word and title
suggestion by TS

-my thanks to TS <g>


## 179. Untitled - 2000.07.13

Like the hummingbird
stopping at every bloom
to sip at raw nectar
the images flicker
across my mind
past my eyes -
a myriad of color.

- concept suggested by TS

## 180. Under Pressure - 2000.07.13

My nerves are raw
as the stress
grates on them
like dissonant notes -
out of tune
and painful to my senses.

As the heat builds outside,
it is like a crock pot -
pressure reading to explode.

And the grasp on
the beating heart tightens -
I am left gasping
for air
as everything
tumbles
downwards.

- title by KS

## 181. Images - 2000.07.13

As dusk falls
and the skies
darken to the mottled purple
I watched the shadows cast
sharpen
then blend
into hidden corners.

-title by KS

## 182. First Sight - 2000.07.14

I first saw you in PVC
and wondered if it were real -
this happiness and bubbly
thoughts
that I think I must now feel

And like the doubter
that I am
I sought to hide
away
only to say sometimes:
I like to see you every day.

-title by KS

## 183. Midnight Moon - 2000.07.14

As the clock
sounds the witching hour
the shine of the night sky
and the silvery moon draw
my eyes to the
heavens above

The stillness of the night
is broken only by
the soft sounds of breathing

The hazy light
that is cast
reveals the soft shadows
that hides us

## 184. The Audience - 2000.07.15

To see your laughter
I will beg and plead,
to lift your spirits
I fall to my knees

For all these things
that I wouldn't for another,
I unthinkingly do
like a mindless druther

In all this
I am confused;
the only goal
for you to be amused

So nicely asked,
how could I refuse?

-title by KS

## 185. Brief Respite - 2000.07.15

The hot summer sun
begs for a cool noon breeze
that runs quickly
through the trees
that surround me.

The grass sways
and then turn silent
as the air moves away
once more.

-title by KS

## 186. Untitled - 2000.07.15

The hazel eyes,
the winsome smile
were all part of your happiness
that I sought to capture
in few words

As you spun around in circles
I realized that you were
still a babe.

## 187. The Candle - 2000.07.15

As the flickering flame
consumed the ice cream,
slowly melting
to a molten white,
the swirl of colors
against the blue flame
became a rainbow.

-title by KS

## 188. Surrender - 2000.07.16

With the softest of glances
it became the lightest of touch
as the darkness of the night
surrendered to the
dawning of the new day.

The briefest of struggles
saw the shifting
from the grey
to a pale peach
as the morning sun
peeked
above the horizon.

-title by KS

## 189. The Race - 2000.07.17

Like the lightning
that runs across the skies,
followed by the low rumble
of thunder,
my mind races
faster than the torrential rains,
seeking to outrun
the questions
that emerge

As the storm stops,
the clouds part
to reveal a sky
pale pink and
bring forth
a new day.

-title by KS

## 190. Adieu - 2000.07.19

It was a babbling brook,
or was it a cascading creek
that carried my thoughts
in paper boats
past the murky depths.

Like the lantern boats
of yesteryear
I free my hopes
and deepest fears
bidding
godspeed,
and bon voyage
to all that I held
in the depths of
my mind.

-title by KS

## 191. Untitled - 2000.07.19

The blazing sun
is followed by the cool night air
as I trace the path
of the stars
against the tapestry
of inky blackness

As my eyes watch
the heavens
I am vividly reminded
of the sunlight
that awaits me
the very next day.

## 192. Perfect Sharing - 2000.07.20

If I sought perfection
what would I really find?

I would not care
for the surface perfection

I would be blind
to her perfect features;
deaf to her
beautiful voice,
and numb to
her softest touch.

I only want
to be able to
share my dreams
and hopes
and
would hope to
hear her's
as well.

-title by KS

## 193. Searching - 2000.07.20

In finding
I am lost

In seeking
I am blind

In wanting
I am numb

Such is the fate
where I can see
but not touch

I can find
but not keep

I can love
but not forever

- title suggested by TC

## 194. Untitled - 2000.07.22

The summer showers
passed quickly
leaving a brilliant rainbow
against a sky of grey.

## 195. Beautiful Day - 2000.07.22

The blaze of the morning sun
reflects against the
shiny mirrored walls
as the dawn sky
is lit to a brilliant
pink
against the faint grey clouds.

Bright orange
against pale blue,
the world awakens
to a beautiful day.

-title by KS

## 196. Untitled - 2000.07.22

If you asked me
why I loved you,
I would have no words
that captures
what I feel
when I see you,
what I think,
when I hear you,
and how I smile
when I think of you.

There would be no picture
that could paint
a brighter laughter;
no day
with a better start
than the times
that I see you in the morning;
and the joy
I carried in the evening.

## 197. Untitled - 2000.07.22

There is no loss greater
than that of love -
given freely
but left to wither.

## 198. Untitled - 2000.07.22

The dark skies
are dotted with white
as the late afternoon sun
does nothing to abate
the cool lake winds.

The few specks of colors
on the waters
are sailing into the
sunset.

## 199. Untitled - 2000.07.22

As the night deepens,
the winds carry our thoughts
to the four corners
of the world.

And with an electric arch,
I watch the lights
decorate the shoreline.

## 200. I close my eyes - 2000.07.23

I closed my eyes
and saw your smile,
I heard the wind
and remembered your voice.

The changing sky
held your eyes
and I watched
fascinated.

When I dream again of today,
I will remember you
and how everywhere I was,
you were too.

-title by KS

## 201. Untitled - 2000.07.23

As the sun sets
in a blaze of golden flame
the evening sky
embraces a darker glory.

The low horizon is filled
with clouds
as a brisk wind carries
my thoughts homeward bound.

## 202. Eyes - 2000.07.24

As the late afternoon sun
reflects on the glass that
surrounds me,
the room gradually warms
and I am reminded
of the cool green of your eyes.

The verdant depths
catching me easier
than any net cast.

And I tumble happily
downwards
if only in hopes
of landing
in a soft embrace.

-title by KS

## 203. Sights of the world - 2000.07.24

The subtle moonlight
reflects the sights of the world
in your eyes.

And like emeralds,
they glisten with happiness
as your laughter peals
across the harrowed fields.

-title by KS

## 204. Relief - 2000.07.26

The late summer heat
makes us yearn
for a shaded tree
and cool drinks.

As the images shimmer
in the heat
I watch the dust clouds
gather
and then disperse
as the first drops of rain
provide a welcome relief.

-title by KS

## 206. Summer Sharing - July 26, 2000

One scoop
two scoop
three scoop
four.

A rainbow of colors
pass my eyes -
they follow the path
of the perfect mounds.

A base of fruit,
a layer of glaze,
two smiles,
one spoon.

-title by KS

## 207. 2000.07.26

Watching the swirling of
white against black -
it melts into a rich
golden brown
as the white crystals
vanish into
the spinning vortex.

A steady stream of white
provides a subtle contrast
to the fragrant scents
that fill our senses.

## 208. Raspberry Jam - 2000.07.27

As the brightly red jam
crossed that brief distance
between spoon and mouth,
a gentle piece gradually
falls
and
the raspberry dribbles
become a sweetly
tantalizing
reward
as my eyes
devour
the path that the crimson
droplets carve
against
the smooth flesh.

## 209. Morning Sun - 2000.07.29

The thick summer heat
envelopes everything
that the morning sun
sees.

The faintest bird songs
are heard
as the last vestiges
of sleep
begins to slip away.

A glance
around the room
reveals that
dawn has already
passed
as the shadows
lengthen.

-title by KS

## 210. Captured - 2000.07.29

looking inside
from without

capturing a moment
for eternity

describe emotion
with mere words

-title by KS

## 211. Cold Heart - 2000.07.30

At two in the morning
the heart runs cold
as the words filter through,
the blood freezes over

As I stay here
rooted in disbelief,
my thoughts are running
away from the words
that have been
etched in my hearing

Like a shadow
in the darkest of nights,
I watch,
with bemused detachment
as I become ice
once more.

-title by KS

212. Verbal Tinder -
2000.07.30

As I sit outside,
I watch the flickering flame
consume the pages
carefully,
devouring the words
like a hunger unchecked.

I continue to tear
each word -
like tinder
feeding it
to the demons
that burn inside
as surely
as the flame
without.

The blazing warmth
does nothing
to assuage
the coldness
within.

-title by KS

213. Sink Like a Stone -
2000.07.30

Like a one hand clap
there is no bottom
in the wellspring
I see

As I begin to drop
the stones
I remember

to tie the emotions
to them
- watching
as they sink
further
and faster
in the depthless
bottom

This continues
until I feel
nothing at all -
empty once again.

-title by KS

214. Untitled - 2000.07.31

The pitter patter of the rain
drops
matches the slow beat of your
heart
as the cool weather outside
emphasizes the warmth within.

The gathering storm
serves to remind me
of the frailty of life,
broken only by the
excitement of the lightning.

## 215. Sunset - 2000.08.01

As the colours drain away
I am left
to look at
the sepia tones
that dominate the land.

As the play of filtered light
and shadowy darkness
resolves itself,
I am left
breathless
at the image
I see.

## 216. Soaked - 2000.08.01

The sudden downpour
catches us unawares
as the thunder rolls
through the heavens.

Even before we can reach
the safety of nearby shelters,
the rain falls
as we are soaked to the skin...

Resisting the urge to run
now that we are dripping wet
we continue
the slow walk
in the rain.

-title by KS

## 217. Intoxicated - 2000.08.01

It was a rich chocolate cake
soaked in brandy
that gave the scent away.

As I watched the blade descend
cutting a neat slice
against a background of white,
layered against ripe cherries.

I saw the wet tongue
slightly circle your lips
as your eyes lit up
in sheer anticipation.

Intoxicated
by the absolute
voluptuousness of the dessert,
your eyes closed
and your face
gains a look of ecstasy
matched only by
few others.

-title by KS

## 218. Red Hot - 2000.08.02

Watching molten gold
move slowly
from spout
to mold.

The sparks fly
as the solid
becomes pliable
once more

As the heat increases
I watch
the colors change
from deep orange
to a brilliant red

The small drops of sweat
gather at the tip
of your smile -
smoldering
as your eyes
glaze over.

-title by KS

## 219. Tranquility - 2000.08.04

The earliest rays of day
carries the cool breezes
of the morning
as
the faintest sounds
of life outside
beckons to us
once again.

The blue sky
is filled only
by the softest shapes
of clouds
as my eyes
soak in
the utter
tranquility
of the moment.

-title by KS

## 220. Syrup - 2000.08.04

The rich golden color
lightens
as a slow and gentle heat
is applied

Melting from a golden drop
to a liquid sweetness,
I watch
as it is drizzled
slowly
against
a toasty surface

The pores absorb
the ambrosia
like
the unquenchable
thirst
of the
desert.

## 221. Untitled - 2000.08.05

The dawn hours
reveal a grey sky
that gradually emerges
to a shade of pink

The heavens surrender
the stars
as the bright sun
outshines
their pale lights.


## 222. Untitled - 2000.08.05

The early morning sun
reveals
the world anew
as sharp shadows
are cast
against the land


## 223. Untitled - 2000.08.05

The crisp harbour breeze
blends with the brilliant skyline
as the busyness of the day
is eased


## 224. Crab Cakes - 2000.08.06

It was the golden brown crust
that lures us in -
a veritable feast for the senses
as the harbour scents
mix in with
the delectable taste
of the offerings of the sea

The only time
where a hard cake
is made from
soft-shelled creatures -
the first taste
is the hook
that catches our hunger
and reels us in

Each small sliver
white-gold as the
cake crumbles easily
to the hungry eyes.

-title by KS

## 225. Baltimore Delight - 2000.08.06

Each sliver of white gold
was followed by the
unending hums of
pleasure
as the taste
was thoroughly
savored.

Each bite was heaven
found on the most
fulfilling of foods

Only after
devouring the first one,
savouring the second,
and truly
experiencing the third,
has the insatiable hunger
assuaged

This unique taste
of fried soft crabs
is indelibly marked
forever
on taste buds
that already yearn
for more.

-title by KS

## 226. Breezes - 2000.08.06

The cool ocean air
pushes the white capped waves
against the shore

The hazy clouds
part to reveal
the moon's
silvery reflection
in the water.

As the night deepens,
the breeze becomes stronger
as nature
begins the race again
to reclaim
the shore.

- title by KS

## 227. Puzzle Piece - 2000.08.07

I heard your voice on the phone
now I had one more piece
to match the puzzle I made
of all the things I knew

As I count the days
to when we meet
I wonder at the picture
I make of
all the things
I knew

-title by KS

## 228. Taffy - 2000.08.07

It was a sweetly salty taste
that reminded me
of the crisp
ocean air
and sandy beaches
of the shore.

A gentle pulling
stretches the pieces
to a translucent
golden brown -
fine enough
that I see through
to the other side

Sticky fingers,
laughing eyes
are all that remains
of this sweet
remembrance.

-title by KS

## 229. The Flame - 2000.08.09

It was a bright blue flame
that burnt
unceasingly,
with an undying hunger
to devour all that
lay between
here
and somewhere else

Looking into the flame,
a center of white was seen -
quickly replaced
by
a brilliant red,
then fiery orange.

The flame burnt
until all that remained
were black ashes -
lifeless soot
that lived no longer.

-title by KS

## 230. Firestorm - 2000.08.10

Like a firestorm
running across the land,
you crossed chasms
and mountains
with the greatest of ease

Burning away old worries
and preparing
for new life
that finds shelter
amongst the cinders
that now dot the forest floor

-title by KS

## 231. Evening Tide – 2000.08.12

The brisk ocean breeze
pushes the white cap waves
towards the shore

The moon is partially hidden
by the hazy clouds
as the boardwalk crowds
fade into the night

The winds grow
in strength
and nature begins
the path
to reclaiming the shores

-title by KS

## 232. Hot - 2000.08.13

At the height of the summer
season
the sun shine is strong -
burning into tanned flesh
mercilessly

The stifling heat
muffles the sounds outside
as the pale drops of sweat
fall downwards

-title by KS

## 233. Waffles a la Mode - 2000.08.13

Cool white ice cream
against a hot
toasty surface
melting slowly
into the pores
of the
freshly made waffle

A light sprinkling
of icing sugar
against
rich gold
disappears
as the trickles
of ice cream
slowly wend their way
through the hot ridges
of each square

-title by KS

## 234. Moonrise - 2000.08.13

As the sun sets to the west
I watch the shadowed
appearance
of the full moon
low against the eastern sky

In the dusky skyline
I am followed by
the sun
as I race
towards the moon.

As dark descends
the wee stars
of the summer nights
make their appearance
against
inky blackness.

-title by KS

## 235. Beckoning Road - 2000.08.16

In half hidden darkness
the road beckons
as we travel
side by side
on a path
that tells a tale
all of its own

In the deep night
I wonder
if the world stands still
when we fall in love
or whether
it spins on
unknowing
of all that
has passed

-title by KS

## 236. Smiling Eyes - 2000.08.17

Every time I looked
you smiled
and
so did I

But only sometimes
did I see
your eyes smile
and those
I treasured most
when your eyes
twinkled
and
my hearted lifted
too.

-title by KS

## 237. The Gift - 2000.08.17

There are few gifts in life
more precious than those
freely given

For what is love
but for a gift
from one heart
to another ?

Even as lives may part
the one gift that remains
will be the memories
that we shared.

- title by KS

## 238. Devotion - 2000.08.17

Every word you whispered
to the wind
I heard
and remembered
like the deepest etchings
on stone

Every dream you had
I held
like gossamer feathers
seeking
to fulfill them all

Every wish you left unsaid
I learnt from others -
all that would make
you happy

-title by KS

## 239. The cooling trend - 2000.08.19

As summer nears an end
the crisp autumn winds
steal away the lingering warmth
from these fleetingly hot days
that are already fading
in our memories

As the verdant colours of
summer
give way to bright reds
and dark gold,
the skies deepen to a grey
in the early morning light
as a faint layer of dew
glistens

- title by KS

## 240. Trying to forget - 2000.08.19

In the night time
where darkness covers the land
I dream
of the times past
where we were just two
amongst millions

our pasts were separate,
our presence together
but our future unknown

And every time I dream now
I remember those days
where my thoughts were
surrounded

by all that you were
and lament the loss

Every night I can only hope
that tomorrow,
begins another day
where I will no longer
dream of you.

-title by KS

## 241. Shattered - 2000.08.19

The four chambers of the heart
shatter so easily
when broken by the slightest word
uttered unfeelingly.

And loneliness
is just one more feeling
that overwhelms me
as I search for
comfort alone

Every time I see you
and think about what we had
I relive
all the memories
that we shared
as we raced
to this precipice
where my heart shattered

- title by KS

## 242. Out of Reach - 2000.08.20

Every time you hurt,
my heart clenches -
not close enough
to help you
but not far enough
to ignore the pain.

And through each word I see
I worry
about you
and rage
at the distance
that separates us.

- title by KS

## 243. Sandstorm - 2000.08.20

In a world of millions
we are alone
blankly looking out
onto the barren desert
that forms the innerscape
of our lives
and like the brisk winds
that run across the desert
you cause the shifting sands
to swirl
and envelope me
once more

- title by KS

## 244. Silent Laughter - 2000.08.20

Empty rooms
match empty hearts
as all I can remember
are the days
we shared
before

The past sounds hollow
as I walk the empty halls
where we once passed each other
in laughter and smiles

Only when I close the doors
does the unending silence
cut through to me

- title by TC, original theme by TC

## 245. Untitled - 2000.08.21

What began
as a grey overcast morning
has gradually changed
to the hot afternoon sun
where the breeze
is felt
only when moving.

Remembering this
as one of the remaining
days of summer
as the drops of sweat
are relentless.

## 246. Sanctuary - 2000.08.24

What separates awareness
and dreams?

Where do our hearts live
when reality is nightmare-like,
that we retreat to the
warmer climes
of past dreams?

Like old wooden boxes
that carry our dreams
when we were young,
so to, do our hearts
remember
all that has passed.

- title by KS

## 247. Fourth Grade Journal - 2000.08.24

First day
of a new year,
under clear skies
reality frees
the
heart once more.

Gathering all that we
really need
and
dream of
every day.

Jotting down
our
unheard thoughts,
reading them
now and then
as the
latent feelings emerge.

## 248. Barbarians - 2000.08.24

Barb is a vision -
always making us smile,
ready to "go there"
based on a single *grin*
as we
read statements like:
I
am
nekkid... we might even
smirk.

## 249. Stacy - 2000.08.24

Starting the Barbarians, it
takes more than just an
ardent fan that
captures the fun
y'all have...

## 250. Karen - 2000.08.24

Keeping an eye on errant
Barbarians
as the playing
resumes, only to be reminded
that it is
ending as the time
nears midnight PDT.

## 251. Troubleshooter - 2000.08.24

Truly
remarkable
offerings of
undeniably
beautiful
love stories -
easily becoming a
salaciously
hilarious
open-hearted
orator of the best
things -
especially when
reading out loud.

## 252. Meleager - 2000.08.25

Most often, his
expressive use of words
leaves us all searching for that
elusive dictionary but it is
always fun and
good to learn forms of
explaining what is
reality...

## 253. Alias - 2000.08.25

Always the
leading cheerleader
in
all things that
say Barbarian *G*

## 254. Harley - 2000.08.25

How often
are we living or are we
really just dreaming of
long rides
every day on
your own motorcycle?

## 255. Untitled - 2000.08.26

Journey through a lifetime and
halfway
around the world, I see the
cascades of sunlight
in the early morning mist,
never before seen until
today but will
always be remembered.

## 256. Lurker Number 1 - 2000.08.26

Lurking is an
unusual skill meant for the most
reticent of pups,
known only by their unending
enthusiasm as the
reigning lurker brigade. *g*

Never before have the
unspoken
masses
become a living
entity in a
room - where they become the
norm.

1 is the number given to the lead
Lurker. *g*

## 257. Sigh - 2000.08.27

A rainy Sunday morning
passes quickly
as the cool autumn breezes
ruffle
the fluttering curtains
only to reveal
wide open eyes
that
close once more
in
muted
satisfaction

-title by KS

## 258. Sweat - 2000.08.27

The summer heat
stifles all life
as I watch
the drops of sweat
slowly run
across
the half-hidden face -
tracing a path
through the
sheen of dust
that covers
every open pore

## 259. Untitled - 2000.08.27

It was a golden honey
against pale flesh
that softly glittered
in the soft
afternoon sunlight

And all my eyes could see
was the writhing of planar flesh
as each drop
was carefully released
downwards

## 260. What is love - 2000.08.28

What is love
but the fleetest of emotions
that betrays the fickle heart...

What is love
but that which is shared between
two hearts

What is love
but all that we search for
in every lifetime lived.

- title by KS

## 261. Untitled - 2000.08.28

Fall evenings
are filled with
cool breezes
that quickly
dries the sweat
of the day hours.

## 262. Unrequited - 2000.08.28

As easily as you stole my heart,
I gave up my words
leaving them
unwritten
and unheard.

For each time
our eyes met,
all my thoughts left me
and my mind
spun around
in desperate attempts
to trace the path
that you traveled
even as I watched you
move away.

-title by TC

## 263. Unconditional Love - 2000.08.29

There are fewer things in life
more precious than
unconditional love -
something given
that asks for nothing
in return.

Often we are searching
too hard
for something
that we have already -
the love of all that surrounds us.

How willing are we
to see with our eyes?
Rather than feel with our hearts
all the love that we are given.

-title by KS

## 264. Untitled - 2000.08.31

I watch transfixed
as the rivulets
of sweat
drips
unheeding
into the soaked bandanna.

## 265. Colours of the Land - 2000.08.31

The hazy days of summer
are followed
silently
by the clear nights
where all we dream of
are the warmth
of autumn fires
as the colours of the land
change
from brilliant greens
to fiery yellows.

- title by KS

## 266. Lazy - 2000.08.31

Cool mornings
give way to bright noon hours
where the fields
are too lazy
to wave in the
slight breeze
that winds its way
southwards.

-title by KS

## 267. Open Window - 2000.08.31

The muted sounds
of children playing
outside
filter
gently through
the open window
as the last days of summer
slip past
like the grains of sand
that mark the passage of time.

Even as the days shorten
and the flocks head southward,
my eyes turn ever westward
to grasp the splendour
of the rolling hills.

- title by KS

## 268. The Voyage - 2000.09.01

As the water flows
towards the ocean
our thoughts travel
ever outwards

And like the eternal presence
of the stars above,
we can only hope
to find and be loved.

Like the sea,
we are surrounded
by tumultuous waves
that challenge our souls
in endless times.

Sailing on a rudderless craft,
hoping for a calm voyage
we have only the heavens
to guide us
knowing that
no matter what –
we have sailed
by our hearts direction.

-title by KS

## 269. Waiting - 2000.09.01

There are fewer souls in this life
sturdier than those
that when given that last straw
upon their worries,
make a broom
to sweep their fears away.

For even through words,
the tension seeps through
and by the barest of restraints
do I put aside that
wild notion
to immediately fly down
and offer the meager comfort
of a hug.

For all that has happened,
life goes on...
and that which was "nothing" in hope,
is now "nothing" in reality...
and the breath that we held
becomes the laughter
of happiness
as this storm too,
passes.

- title by TC

## 270. Tides of Time - 2000.09.03

Like the seven stages of living
I watch the passage of time
weave its way through our lives
leaving nothing untouched

And I watch
with worldly amusement
as the tides of time
wash against the shore
once more.

- title by KS

## 271. One Day at a Time - 2000.09.03

All of our tomorrows are a new day
where we remember our past
and look to our future

And like a white page
we begin once more
living each day
anew - making our marks
on those around us

All throughout the lifetime
we live one day at a time;
only at the end
will we ever know
if we have touched the minds
of others;
and whether we live through
their memories.

- title by KS

## 272. Slumber - 2000.09.04

In the wee hours,
I listen to the
quiet breaths
of a world asleep
as I watch
the stars
tell me their stories
of the past.

Even as the night deepens,
the faint summer breezes
rustle the leaves
and I watch
the world turn over
once more
and sleep again.

- title by KS

## 273. The Moment - 2000.09.04

The moment
that separates
slumber and awareness
is but one breath
that the world holds -
pure silence
as everything stops for
no reason
except to meet
the coming dawn.

- title by KS

## 274. Pup Bar - 2000.09.04

What began
as a room
of strangers
has grown
to a small Bar
of patrons
where we share
their worries,
their sorrows
and their happy times.

Linked by the initial bond,
it grows until
we are sharing
one more common bond -
the friendships we make.

- title by TC

## 275. Last Day of Summer - 2000.09.04

The cool lake breeze
quickly dries the sweat
that gathers
in a salty pool

Bright sunlight,
dappled shadows
amongst the large oak trees
makes for
one last day of summer
as autumn
peaks around the corner.

- title by KS

## 276. Fall - 2000.09.04

The evening breeze
leaves a chill in the air
as the sun dips
below the horizon

The drop in warmth
reflects the loss
of summer days
as the fall months
approach us.

- title by KS

## 277. Magnetic - 2000.09.05

The half moon -
I see it tonight
and imagine
that you may
have glanced once
at the halves
you saw last night.

And like the oceans
that are swayed
by the moon,
I find myself
being pulled in
by your magnetic eyes

As the night passes,
your hold wanes
until I sleep -
where once more
you've captured
my thoughts

- title by KS

## 278. Raw Honey - 2000.09.07

The taste of raw honey
has a tang that lingers
on the tongue
even as we reach for
another drop

Bright gold in the morning sun,
it twists ever so slightly
before gathering
in one perfect drop
that lands carefully
on your lips

- title by S

## 279. Cookies and Cream - 2000.09.09

My attention was caught
by the rhythm
of short hard nibbles
against a dome of white
and as time passed
it became
long, slow licks
along the side,
with each passing
I watch a bright red tongue
drag itself
across the
rapidly melting tip

It is a sweetly
sticky mess
that is made
as the last remnants of ice cream
melt across the fingers.

## 280. Fall and Autumn - 2000.09.09

Fragrant scents
abound as the
leaves float gently, only to
land on the forest floor.

As the lingering summer warmth
unfolds,
the feeling of
untold stories lingers as our
many adventures are
now forgotten

## 281. The Cycle - 2000.09.09

In the early autumn season
the weather cools enough
that the mornings carry
a slight tang of frost,
as the foggy mist of dawn
fades to reveal a rainbow
against the dull colors
of the trees

Once more, the cycle begins
again
as we watch
the land begin its sojourn
to sleepy awareness.

- title by KS

## 282. The Flame - 2000.09.10

The pure blue flame
captures the color of your eyes
in a perfect moment
before a slight twist
of the wrist reveals
a crimson red
that is matched only
by the shade upon your lips

And like the flame
that you so resemble,
a burning possession
that consumes all that lays
along the path,
all my thoughts
have melted again.

- title by TC

## 283. Pathway - 2000.09.11

The brilliant sight
hangs low in the evening sky
as the clouds reveal
a moon
that tinges closer to orange
than true white.

With only the stars
and pale moonbeams
to light a pathway
between here
and eternity,
the silent night
beckons for us
to feel once more.

- title by KS

## 284. Intersection - 2000.09.13

Spinning freely
is the puzzle
we strive to solve
over a lifetime
of living -
to find the
other half of
our souls
before our
time runs out.

Two trains,
two lives,
two boats,
two lovers,
all pass through the night
and by the merest of chance
do they ever meet
along the same line.

- title by KS

## 285. Life's River - 2000.09.13

A frail grasp
is all that we have
on this river
that we call life ~
clinging
by the meanest of hopes
onto those
that would have
left our hand
had we
forsaken ourselves
to the torrential
flow.

Held closely,
we seize upon
hope, love and laughter
as the support
as we careen
wildly
down the river.

-title by TC

## 286. Celestial Conga Line... - 2000.09.14

As the clouds part
in the evening sky,
I look up to see the
bright beauty of the
heavens
as the stars
gather in a royal
train,
following the path
of the Moon.

- title by KS

## 287. Remembering - 2000.09.14

Like the smallest drops
of the deepest oceans
our memories
are all that binds us
to this life.

As no step in a river
is ever the same,
there is no memory
that does not change.

Only by walking along the shores
to remember our days by the
ocean
do we make a lasting
impression
on the shifting sands.

- title by KS

## 288. Chocolate Cherry Cake - 2000.09.15

It's a sweet dark glaze
that slowly covers
the porous cake -
filling every
nook and cranny,
wending their way
between the layer of cherries
that lay snug between
thick
heavy
slabs
of chocolate cake.

The rich scent
wafts along the current
as eyes watch
avidly
that
first
bite
that is followed
by
another...
slowly.

## 289. The First Step - 2000.09.15

On all that roads that we ever travel
the first step takes us
upon a journey
into the beyond
that we could never
trod again.

Like the heavens
in their vastness,
my dreams pull me
beyond the present
and into the future.

Like the millions of stars
that I cannot see,
the roads I travel
spread beyond
the horizon.

- title by KS

## 290. Transitions - 2000.09.18

The faintest of haze
envelopes the sky
as the sun begins
its final journey
beyond the clouds

Even as autumn
peers around the corner
the rays of sunlight
are relentless
but quickly diminish
as night creeps
into the city.

We are buffeted
by cool winds
that hearken
to the darkest days
of winter.

- title by KS

## 291. Mental Vacation - 2000.09.18

As the autumn night darkens
the half moon rises,
and my thoughts
chase themselves
across the skies
to a place
where sunshine
and warmth
are the norm.

- title by KS

## 292. Brief - 2000.09.19

It was that one moment
in time
where our eyes met
and hearts began to beat
in the same rhythm

It was the briefest
second passed,
and the one time I
remember forever.

Like the arches of lightning
that lit the sky,
the slender contact
of one smile
against
another
remains
unforgotten.

- basis on a word: "briefing/brief"
- TS

## 293. The Dance - 2000.09.19

Along a smooth layer of gold,
I watch the sliver of dark brown
sinuously play,
wending itself
against two edges that
push
the chocolate slowly
against itself.

The swirling dance
of dark against light
ends only
as I watch the knife
descend against
the edge -
only to stop
for one
timeless moment
as the world
stops
to breathe...
and slice once more.

- title by KS

## 294. Absolute... - 2000.09.20

In a world of uncertainty,
there is no absolute
that we can cling to,
and like a riverboat
that floats lazily along
the Mississippi,
we drift
until the turbulence
of the water
tosses our lives
into the swirling eddies
of confusion.

- word from S

## 295. Berries - 2000.09.20

The fresh blue
globes
tumble lightly
over a moist
white slope
where they land
in pools of sweetness

Followed by a gentle
flood of red
raspberries
that dimpled the
slippery cream

The honey glaze
gathers at the base of
the cream as I watch
the fruit gather
on the edge
of whiteness.

- title by KS

## 296. Balance - 2000.09.22

The delicate balance
between light and dark
hinges upon the strength
that we find within ourselves
to guide our lives
beyond the day to day.

It needs but one word,
one thought,
one moment in time
where life
and death
are but a breath apart.

Like the meekest of candles,
in the morning dawn,
faintly seen in the distance,
that one point
remains the reason
why we continue
to walk the road
into the rising sun.

- title by KS

## 297. Medley - 2000.09.23

A medley of black currants,
blueberries and ripe
raspberries lay covered
the sweetest of sauces

A shimmering layer of brown
sugar
and crisp oats
are baked until golden

Sprinkled gently
on the last offerings of
the summer bounty,
it forms a delicate contrast
to the senses.

- title by S

- very berry crisp

## 298. Thanksgiving - 2000.09.24

As the fall weather cools,
the land turns a golden hue
that casts the world
and our eyes to
the coming of winter months.

A gathering of friendly faces
by the hearth
leads to hours
of happy conversation
and mirth.

Cranberries, sweet sauce
and the fragrant scent
of tradition cast
our memories back.

We give thanks
for the bountiful spread
that lay before us ~
and keep in our thoughts
the lives of those
less fortunate.

- title by KS

## 299. Hurting - 2000.09.26

In the face of unbearable loss,
what do you say to another?
How do you listen to the
whispers
of sympathy,
when you want to howl at your
pain?

Where does the pain end
and memories begin?
As the world staunchly marches
on,
our lives spin out of control,
and our hearts
reel from the hurt
that lays beyond
the next bend.

- title by KS

## 300. Goodbye - 2000.09.26

Even as the summer
memories bid us
fond farewell,
I look to the times
of evening walks
as the fledgling flocks
begin their flight
to warmer climes.

- title by KS

## 301. Close My Eyes - 2000.09.28

Close my eyes
and I dream of
green orbs that
look out to the world.

Close my eyes
and I see
a smile
that traverses
ten thousand miles

Close my eyes
and I drift
along a white cloud
to a place where
the only warmth
is from the sun
and the only breeze
is from the rustling
of green leaves.

- title by KS

## 302. Breakdown - 2000.09.28

It was one smile
that crossed the divide
of a lifetime.

It was one touch
that broke the frozen
prison
our lives were locked in.

It was one look
that melted the walls
that surround
the heart.

- title by KS

## 303. The Journey - 2000.09.29

From beginning to end,
we travel life's path as a journey
that our hearts and souls
would learn and grow.

From start to finish,
we look forward in anticipation,
and to our past in memory,
as we run this race to eternity.

From now until forever,
we hope that the road we travel,
is not alone, but with the friends
who join us on the way.

- title by KS

## 304. Wishes - 2000.09.29

If wishes were stars,
then no more
would there be
sad songs in bars.

If wishes were horses,
then the races
would no longer be fun
but just "of course's."

But as surely as dawn
falls the dark,
luck and wishes
are just that -
gifts to the unsuspecting,
turning up at
just the right moment.

- title by KS

## 305. Good Morning - 2000.10.02

The autumn breeze
causes a flicker in
the blustery flag,
as the morning sun
warms our hearts
as much as it does
our bodies.

- title by KS

## 306. Beignettes - 2000.10.02

It's a crisp golden twist
of light fluffiness
that one never forgets -
always remembering
the taste
of the white sugar
against cinnamon -
a fragrant scent
that wafts
all the way from
the Quarters
where the open
cafés are -
sunlight
and conversation
are the order
of the day.

## 307. The Traveler - 2000.10.09

Slicing through the heavens,
we turn our eyes upwards
to gaze upon the stars.

Between the clouds below,
we see the lights reflected
in the cities upon the land.

Even as we travel quickly,
our thoughts are ever faster -
already landing
in the embrace
of the ones we love.

-title by KS

## 308. The Clarion - 2000.10.10

Midnight songbirds
with clear crisp tones
that reverberate
through the darkness...

Like a clarion at dawn,
it draws me once more
to listen
and to savour
all that is sung.

-title by KS

## 309. The Search - 2000.10.11

The unending road
travels beyond
the next horizon
as our paces
bring us ever closer
to the journey
that begins
and ends
with our souls.

Reaching for the moonlight
that gathers in pools
and light the way
of the stars,
our minds travel
faster than
the swiftest of birds.

Knowing that loneliness
is the only reason
that keeps our journey
undying
as we search
for the other half
of our soul.

-title by KS

## 310. Untitled - 2000.10.15

Like the gentlest raindrops
against worn stone,
the lilting voice
takes me one more step
towards slumber.

- Sweet Slumber - CS

## 311. Waiting - 2000.10.18

All throughout our lives
we are told
that there's another -
someone "out there"
that is "just" for us...

All throughout our lives
we live alone
in the dark
waiting for something
that seems
just beyond our reach...

All throughout our lives,
we are alone,
because the promise
of another life
is just that -
a promise.

-title by KS

## 312. The Push - 2000.10.18

What moves us to begin
the journey
that leads us from
here until
ever after
is the same
force
that propels us
to dream
and to dare to reach for
those hopes.

-title by KS

## 313. Alive - 2000.10.18

Every breath we take
begins another moment
that we live -
another chance
that we take -
betting on living
more than just
being.

Every day we live,
we move on with all
that is important to us;
spending time with all
that we treasure.

-title by KS

## 314. Voice Recognition - 2000.10.19

It was voice to match the face
that I had only seen from afar,
a sound to carry
the thoughts across an ocean,
a cadence
that danced across a smile.

For every moment that passed,
the musical octaves
reflected the depth
that I had read once before.

-title by KS

## 315. The Power - 2000.10.20

For all the belief
in the powers of the world,
it begins
from within -
for by the grace
of our dreams,
our hopes,
and our fears -
we strive
to make them real.

-title by KS

## 316. Brass Ring - 2000.10.20

It was dark silk against
alabaster
as I watch the gentle curtain
of soft strands
fall to the nape
of your neck -
hiding the delectable skin
from a searching mouth.

Like the feel of velvet
against cool marble,
the gentle gliding
of fingertips
against soft skin
brings a slight smile
to red lips.

-title by KS

## 317. Priceless - 2000.10.22

Genuine emotion
is one of the few things
that we should be so lucky to
find
and keep forever.

In a time where superficial is the
norm
and depth measured by seconds
together
and not the time we pine apart,
true concern - how do we
recognize it
for what it is?

A truth more beautiful
than the night sky
bedecked with a million
sparkling jewels.

-title by KS

## 318. Laundry Day - 2000.10.25

The low rumble
in the background
is a soothing hum
as I watch the world
go by in cycles.

With all the worries
bubbling away
to be washed out
in another load
of silly soap flakes
that bubble over
and draw laughter
from the reluctant
washers.

-title by KS

## 319. The Search - 2000.10.26

In waiting,
we find love;
while finding,
we wait.

Like the balance
that we search for,
love begins -
from within,
and searches -
from without.

Looking,
finding,
keeping,
sharing...

-title by KS

## 320. Pearl - 2000.10.29

The clear glisten
on the pearl
is a salt water glaze
that caresses
the brightly sheened jewel,
nestled in two filliped halves
that buffer the harsh world
from the comforts of within.

-title by KS

## 321. Phoenix Rising - 2000.10.31

As the phoenix rises
beyond the ashes of each life,
it searches
for the reason it returns
to the cycle of living,
striving always to reach
a pinnacle
that it could not
before.

It is the heavy tail-feathers
that give the bird
its beauty,
and the balance for flight.

Each rebirth calls for a change,
each flight demands a new
ending.

Every fiery death
sheds another layer of our past
until we look only forwards.


## 322. Winter's Warmth - 2000.11.02

The late sunshine
casts warm shadows
against cool windows
as the sharp sunlight
is foiled against
the naked branches
that line the streets.

As the flocks begin
their flight to lands
far away - where summer
warmth beckons.

-title by KS


## 323. Giggle Giggle - 2000.11.05

Jiggle jiggle
yellow jello

Jiggle jiggle
mellow fellow

Jiggle jiggle
worm squirms

jiggle jiggle
wish fish

jiggle jiggle
sun fun

jiggle jiggle
man ran

jiggle jiggle
late date

jiggle jiggle
wriggle giggle

jiggle jiggle
sigh, bye.

-title by KS

## 324. Inspiration - 2000.11.08

Silence is golden
only if it's broken
by the soft sounds
that is music to my ears.

Every turn that marks a new day
brings together my thoughts
on a clean page.

And the words fall downwards
onto a sheet of white,
it jumps
from line to line
where
it slides across the page
like marbles after break.

-title by KS

## 375. Globes - 2000.11.08

Sweet, succulent globes
of firm flesh
that beckon
for the bite
that leaves them
glistening in the sunlight.

Each nibble reveals
a crimson wine stain
against dark skin
that draws
the sweet juice
once more.

Each globe becomes
an experience on their own,
as eyes watch
the shrinking number of
grapes
on the vine

- title by S

## 376. Contrasts - 2000.11.10

The slight folds
on the surface
draws our eyes
to the stray nubbin
that remains
on the pale surface.

Dark red against
smooth white,
the careful circling
of the malleable
tip against
the mound of ice cream
as the warm
suction
slowly molds
the hot raisin
against cool
cream.

-title by KS

377. Edge of Dreams -
2000.11.12

Darkness rising
against the light
of a silver moon.

Casting a hazy shadow
against frosted windows.

Warm pillows
against
cool floors
as we take shelter
from the biting cold.

Sleep is but a moment
away
as comfort beckons us
to dream
once more.

- title by K

378. Snowscape - 2000.11.17

The chilly night air
gently tosses the snowflakes
hither and fro
as they land against
panes of glass -
creating
a brief snowscape
that quickly disappears
even as the warmth within
melts away.

Darkness descends rapidly
as the cool embrace
of the night
sends light
into hiding
once more.

The snow falls faster
as the street lamps
cast a pale glow
and I watch
the brisk travels
of millions of flakes
cross the golden
river
of light.

-title by KS

379. Oysters - 2000.11.19

On a half shell
surrounded by crystalline ice
glistening in the sun
are a neat half dozen.

Sliding,
slipping,
down the sides
to a waiting maw
that inhales
and devours
every moment
and tidbit
of
the offerings
from the sea.

-title by KS

## 380. Champagne - 2000.11.19

The golden liquid
slides gently down
the slender throat;
cascading
in a flurry of
ticklish waves
as
silvered laughter
is heard...

-title by KS

## 381. The Dance - 2000.11.20

The wild Chinook winds
jettison the flakes
in swirling eddies
against pitch black skies
as the streetlights
cast an unearthly glow
for this wintry dance.

Faster and faster
the snowflakes dance -
a million whirling dervishes
that take us
into another land
of whiteness.

-title by KS

## 382. Pathway - 2000.12.01

like a spot of quicksilver
held against the blue sky
sliding against the edge

tantalizing images of
wandering roads
against paths
carved into rolling hills

the cool spring air
and the scent of rain
is chased away
by the soft afternoon sun

-title by KS

## 383. Hidden Moment - 2000.12.03

A golden song
by voice through time,
I see them move.

Every day passes
wholly treasured,
a hidden moment in time.

Unexpected pleasure mixed
with surprise
of a smile.

-title by KS

## 384. Home Fires - 2000.12.06

Winter darkness
drives us inwards
to the fires hearth
where warmth
is shared amongst
those closest to us.

In the dying days
of autumn, we are left
lamenting
the passage of time,
as we prepare
for long cold nights.

-title by KS

## 385. Yum - 2000.12.06

Slick smooth textures
slide along soft lips
golden against dark red,
as each taste
disappears
with a hum of happiness

-title by KS

## 386. A Million Dreams - 2000.12.10

I saw a million dreams today
float towards the Earth;
landing gently
against the mirrored
surface
and melt away
to become
a million pools
of water

The flurry of motion
that they became
swirling amongst
the lights
as we set
all our dreams and
all our hopes,
once more into flight.

-title inspired by KD

## 387. Sunshine - 2000.12.14

Silkened petals
of wet dew
glisten
in the morning sun

Gather
in the warmth
of the soft haze
that surrounds us

A glaze
dipped in rich honey
covered
with a fine dust
of gold

Basking
in the sunshine
of your laughter.

-title by KS

## 388. Barb Beer - 2000.12.14

The glass throat beckons
like a hollow altar
of wanting

Its emptiness
yearns
for a fulfillment
of the fluid
senses.

Each sip
begets another
as an endless thirst
is quenched.

- titled by various Barbarians

## 389. Paper Cuts - 2000.12.17

The quiet twinges of pain -
a thousand paper cuts to the
soul -
each one not enough to draw
blood
but the feeling persists
nonetheless

The grey skies
match the innerscape of
the barren winter -
relieved only by
the gentle snowfall
from the north.

-title by KS

## 390. Life Unlived - 2000.12.17

Across the distance
of ten thousand miles
the songs of a lifetime
die unsung

In the darkest hours of the
night,
slim moonlight casts pale
shadows
against the empty walls

Mindless warbling drowns out
the crystalline purity
of the voice unheard
and a soul dies -
life unlived

-title by KS

## 391. Loneliness - 2000.12.19

Darkness descends like a shroud
enveloping all that would excite -
a deafening well of silence
provides
slim solace
to the emptiness
that is.

The hollow bleakness
that beckons
to the shadowy confines
in loneliness
once more.

-title by KS

## 392. Riptide - 2000.12.20

Inside out,
twisting in the wind,
floating on the knowledge
of instability.

Upside down,
swimming against the currents,
that sweeps wildly
against the riverside.

Awake yet dreaming,
moving through the tide
that shifts our balance
elsewhere in the sand.

Motionless movement,
making a path amongst stones
that become the steps
towards the shore.

-title by KS

## 393. Winter Solstice - 2000.12.21

The shortest day
and the longest night
passes slowly
as souls gather
once more
around the fire
to hold the chill
at bay.

Once more
into the new year
we cast our hopes forward
and treasure
the memories
of the year just past.

-title by KS

## 394. Glances - 2000.12.22

The chance exchange
of the eyes
in the night
as everyone
hurries home,
toward an evening
of gatherings.

A twinkle of laughter
brightens your eyes
as cold puffs of air
cross your lips.

Eyes meet once more
as our paths slide
together again.

- concept from TC
- title by KS

## 395. Sound of Angels - 2000.12.23

In a city of millions,
I heard a voice today -
clear silvered tones
that carried above
the hum of the masses.

Turning against
the crush of the crowd
craning back
to catch another glimpse
of smiling eyes.

The sound of angels
in the midst of the season
where whiteness
means more than just snow.

-title by KS

## 396. Footprints of Angels - 2000.12.25

The snow falls silently,
cascading down the branches
to land gently
against the frosted windows.

As the night air cools,
sound becomes a slow echo
between the peals of church bells
and the gathering of souls.

Are these footprints of angels
that I spy -
faint against the white ground
watching us all from afar...

-title by KS

## 397. Cold - 2000.12.25

Crisp snow,
clear icicles,
and shimmering pines
cast sharp shadows
against the frozen ground.

Short puffs of cool air
mix with the gleam of your smile
warming the night air quickly,
as our palms rub together for
heat.

-title by KS

## 398. Here I Am - 2000.12.28

Sitting in a lightless room,
sleeping a deathless dream,
seeking the unthinkable,
wanting the undreamt.

-title by KS

## 399. Death - 2000.12.28

Death is a solace that comes unsought
reflecting through the sheen
of a thousand pearls
cascading
through the pain of a thousand lives

-title by KS

## 400. The Lonely Path - 2000.12.28

Travel the lonely path
of the unwanted,
find the thorns of
hate that seem
intent on causing
just a bit more pain
than expected.

Words flow unbidden
through the valley
of shadows.

Every moment,
every step marked
by lost dreams.

-title by KS

## 401. Keeping It In - 2000.12.28

Late is the hour,
dull is the pain
cutting away
through molten butter.

Swallow once, twice,
keeping it in ~
finding the quiet place
once more.

-title by KS

## 402. Ironic - 2000.12.28

Ironic to live by the word,
die by the word,
the soul is cut away -
a slice at a time
by neglect, by indifference
moving in rote motion
through the actions of
the day.

Yes. No. I understand.
No changes in the day,
no feelings felt, if ever.

-title by KS

## 403. The Price I Pay - 2000.12.28

When asked -
was Santa good to you
this year -
how do you tell them yes
and no -
I wanted peace - and
I got it,
it just didn't last
very long
and the price I was paying
outweighs
the visceral joy
that I might have had.

A price that I pay
time and again,
even as the returns
are diminishing.

-title by KS

## 404. The Cycle - 2001.01.06

The pain arcs from
one point to another
lightning catching
on the ends of the
lancing nerves.

A twisting motion
sends another pang
of cold frisson
down taut nerves.

An endless cycle
of hot, cold, hot cold.

The ice never melts
fast enough to really
fade away.

So it is
a frozen barrier
outside and within.

-title by KS


## 405. Resignation - 2001.01.06

It's a slow mixture,
of grief and endless rage
mixing in a quiet pool
of resignation.

Breath in,
breathe out,
let the words wash away,
carved in the memory of me.

The jaws clench in pain
and the lights fade away.

-title by KS


## 406. Patience - 2001.01.06

Patience, like death,
is welcome -
embraced by the weary soul.

Letting go,
and falling into
the abyss of darkness,
taking meek comfort
at frail warmth.

-title by KS


## 407. Eternal Soldier - 2001.01.06

How ironic that
the body is weary,
but the mind struggles on.

Like the eternal soldier,
fighting an endless battle
between destiny
and the reality that beckons.

-title by KS

## 408. Battle - 2001.01.06

Every word is like a cut,
peeled away from the flesh
until it stands alone
in the bitter cold
that buffets the island.

An endless struggle
for the meaning of living,
for the reason to do battle.

-title by KS

## 409. Every - 2001.01.10

Every time
is a new world
of cold darkness,
where dreams don't
cross the threshold,
and warmth finds no shelter.

Every night
is a road less traveled,
wandering the hidden mazes
that shield the world
from me.

Every day
begins anew -
the dark coldness
retreating into
the sunshine
of the day.

-title by KS

## 410. The Pond - 2001.01.16

The glass surface
ripples as the soft sunlight
dances through.

A gentle wind blows off
the silvered waters
as the shallow reeds
bend against their stalks.

A haunting cry
from a hidden loon
breaks the gentle silence.

A flurry of feathers
is all that is seen.

-title by KS

## 411. Sweet Pools - 2001.01.16

Sweet pools of sweat
gather at the nape
of your neck.

Like a snowflake
from the heavens,
falling onto hot flesh -
melting away
on heated warmth.

-title by KS

## 412. Bush or Gore - 2001.01.18

My fascination I abhor
watching my southern friends,
vote for Bush or Gore.
My fascination I abhor
reading newscasts more and more
about an election that would never end.
My fascination I abhor
for the words of "Gore in Four."

Bush or Gore was the cry all year,
playing political games for months on end -
a relentless campaign built on fear.
Bush or Gore was the cry all year,
so many days of wails and tears -
was it Gore or was it Bush? Will America ever mend?
Bush or Gore was the cry all year,
playing political games for months on end.

-title by KS

## 413. Village Idiot - 2001.01.19

The village idiot came to rule,
just thinking us all silly fools.
How could he split the vote school?
The village idiot came to rule!

Four more years of a shrubby fool,
almost makes me cry and drool.
The village idiot came to rule,
just thinking us all silly fools.

-title by KS

## 414. Hail to the Chief! - 2001.01.20

Hail to the Chief!
And swear in number 43 they did today.
Stole election, he's a thief!
Hail to the Chief!

If you have a beef, take it to the Chief!
Maybe he'll say: hey, hey, no way!
Hail to the Chief!
And swear in number 43 they did today.

-title by KS

## 415. Acid - 2001.01.21

Each drop of acid drips,
falls,
and hisses as it lands
on the iron will
that is the only thing
holding together
the pale remnants
of a soul long gone.

Slowly dissolving
onto a surface
long scarred with
the acidic carvings
of an unrelenting
harangue -
vitriol more poisonous
than the vilest
of tortures.

-title by KS

## 416. Emptiness - 2001.01.24

As night deepens
and the shadows soften in the
moonlight
the howls of the wind outside
disappear
into the gaping silence within.

The emptiness
consumes all thoughts
that might have been
silent echoes.

Realization
sinks like a leaden stone
falling faster and faster
into a bottomless maw.

-title by KS

## 417. Silent Pearls - 2001.01.24

Silent pearls falling
against ground silk
soaked in salty wetness.

A somnolent flame
that burns within,
consuming all
that might have been.

-title by KS

## 418. Red - 2001.01.24

The year begins red -
red pearls
against pale silk -
seeping into all
the nooks and crannies
that hid the red lines
from the sight of mortal eyes.

Flowing silently to
mix with the cooling
ice water
that surrounds me.

Dissolving into
a pale pinkish-ness -
a shadow of its
former self.

Mixing amongst the
cold comfort
before disappearing
once more.

-title by KS

## 419. Happy New Year? - 2001.01.24

Red paper, gold leaf,
and the year begins
with a nigh desperate
hope for peace
and solitude,
none of which
are granted.

To be here but for the grace of God,
to live here
but for the grace of someone
beyond me.

Drifting away in a sea of ice,
floating from afar,
dreaming of the empty page
where the water is clear
and the weather cool.

Solitude - sought
but never found.

Is it time yet?

-title by KS

## 420. Winter - 2001.01.31

The grey skies are a bleak foil
for the cool raindrops
that scatter against
the silvered surface.

The howling winds
batter against the warmth
that emanates
from the winter hearth -
once more blazing
comfort to the winter thaws.

-title by KS

## 421. Heart and Soul – 2001.02.02

Heart and soul -
what's one without the other?

Heart and soul -
how do you have one but not
the other?

Heart and soul -
food for the soul;
is comfort for the heart.

Today the heart,
tomorrow the soul,
in the end,
it becomes the whole...

title by TC

## 422. Unrelenting - 2001.02.02

The snowflakes
that descend from the skies -
a heart shatters
into a million pieces.

And like the tears that fall
unrelenting
the heartbreak
reverberates
between now
and eternity.

-title by KS

## 423. Hidden - 2001.02.02

Hidden against a sky of grey
is a sheen of empty raindrops
that splatter aimlessly
against cold windows.

Sheltered by weak shadows
is the empty coldness
that holds no heat.

Acting like a snowflake
that really is a false raindrop,
running endlessly
towards the finish,
only to splash
against nothingness.

-title by KS

## 424. Dancing Shadows - 2001.02.03

The sunlight does a wild dance
between the shadowed corners -
rapidly moving between
light and dark.

Night and day -
a solemn waltz
between
two opposites -
a flame and its shadow.

- title by TC

## 425. Two Lives - 2001.02.04

When does one plus one
equal one?

Where do two lives converge
to become one again?

When two hearts break
how do you count the tears?

How many times
will you name the fears
that haunt your dreams?

Where do two lives
leave the road of solitude
to meet at the point
of togetherness?

Why do two lives
struggle to stay together
even as they part ways?

- title by TC

## 426. Until - 2001.02.04

Close my eyes
and I dream of you -
shy smile
and that twinkle
in your eyes...

- until all I can remember
are the soft words
whispered on the winds;

- until all I can hear
are the summer breezes
that carry your smile
back to me;

- until all I can feel
is the phantom touch
that causes me to reach out
and discover the slow swaying
of the flowers outside.

- title by TC

## 427. Tell Me - 2001.02.05

tell me again
why I watch people?
tell me why
I sit by the side?
tell me
how many times people will get hurt
tell me
the answers I'm trying to find.
don't mind my useless rambling.

-title by KS

## 428. One Day at a Time - 2001.02.07

I remind myself daily
that one day at a time
I must survive one day at a time.

I won't look towards tomorrow
because I must survive today.

That's what is keeping me here -
one day at a time.

I'm beyond the low hum
I hear constantly,
I remind myself -
one day at a time.

I'll never see tomorrow
if everything ends today

So that is my goal tonight
to just live one day at a time.

The throbbing pain
will go away
as I take it one day
at a time.

A dreamless death,
a deathless dream -
maybe I'll sleep today,
as I try to live
one day at a time.

Slow detachment,
and the ice floes
leave once more.

-title by KS

## 429. Walking in the Rain - 2001.02.09

As the evening hours fade
with the dim moonlight,
the hazy mist casts
a pale glow
on two figures
that walk in the light rain.

Heads bent together -
there is no hurry
in escaping
the falling raindrops.

A slow walk
in the rain
ends with
a soft embrace
in a shadowed doorway.

-title by KS

## 430. Snowflakes - 2001.02.10

The winter winds swirl
the snowflakes
in a frenzied dance
that sparkles
in the dying sunlight

A graceful dance
of moonlight and darkness
emerges
as the crystalline forms
settle down
to freeze
from the winds.

-title by KS

## 431. Real? - 2001.02.11

Real-
how do I create form
from mere shadows?
how do I describe laughter
heard once
but felt a million times?

Real -
the moments I draw on
to remember forever
are the times
of your laughter
and happiness.

Real -
is the shade of green
that tinges your eyes;
the shine that I see
in glowing orbs -
even as the camera captures
that moment and nothing more.

Real -
what separates the phantom
touch
from reality -
even now,
my thoughts travel a million
miles
to be with you.

- title by TC

## 432. Transition - 2001.02.13

Daydreamer -
sunshine and warmth
are the only things
I can remember.

Laughter and smiles
are what I have left
from the day
as I switch over
to dreaming at night.

-title by KS

## 433. Captured - 2001.02.13

Chasing across the land
following a blazing hot sun -
basking in the warmth
of your happiness
watching your dancing smile
and sparkling eyes.

Once more,
I capture everything
in a picture
etched forever
on my mind.

-title by KS

## 434. H -> T - 2001.02.13

H
immediately
jostling for a place to
kneel in the presence of a
lovely lady,
moved beyond words
nearly speechless at the
opulence that surrounds her
most
precious
querida
relinquishing her hand only to
savour the sight of
T

## 435. Measurement - 2001.02.13

The distance
that separates "here"
from "there"
becomes
unbearable
as the time flies quickly.

The time that lies
between "now" and
"then" stretches
out to eternity
even as the minutes
fly away.

The thoughts
that separate "you"
from "me"
merge into
a continuous
stream of consciousness.

-title by KS

## 436. Sky Trains - 2001.02.13

Even as the light
dwindles and fades,
the stars appear
in the dark expanse of
black silk.

Casting our thoughts
to the millions
of shining lights
that dot the heavens,
we send our dreams
to ride the trains
in the skies -
carrying our deepest
hopes to the ends
of the world.

-title by KS

**437.** Sheen of White -
2001.02.17

The unrelenting snow fall
blankets everything in sight
leaving out the trees
and rooftops a sheen of white.

Soon, the snow melts
from the warm Earth,
and fades away
to become a puddle.

-title by KS

**438.** Universal Thoughts -
2001.02.19

All throughout our lives, we are
but searching for a
common bond that links us to
those
dearest to us in an
ephemeral thought.

Freely
given, and
heartily sought,
for the moments of
joy.

Knowing
laughter resounds through
my mind,
now more than ever,
original joy.

Precious time that speaks more
for
quality than all that one
requires -
solid
trust is what keeps us alive.

Universal thoughts that
very seldom
waver - with only one
exact answer -
yes... and from here to there...
Zoom! is what you'd hear.

-title by KS

**439.** What you are -
2001.02.19

In a land separated by miles,
you have a map,
to find all roads
may lead to love.

In a world where the blind
can see,
and lovers are apart,
search for wonder
from within the soul.

What you are,
is more than the sum
of all things given.

What you are,
is more than
all things written.

## 440. Silent thoughts... - 2001.02.21

A quarter century is not quite enough
to have lived a life
but to see all the lives
that pass me by.

It's not quite enough to inure me
to the pain that swirls
in the lives
of those around me.

Twice I have witnessed
the shattering of lives
and once more
I will see.

I am the silent watcher from afar.

## 441. The Call - 2001.02.22

Like the softest snow of
December,
falling,
melting away on a breeze,
the gentle voice
carries us off
into the setting sun
of southern climes.

Peals of laughter
capture the moment -
and the heart
with unimaginable ease -
holding without keeping;
finding without seeking.

-title by KS

## 442. Believe - 2001.02.22

The question you might ask...is:
are they or aren't they,
and why people could never say
yea or nay...

So to begin this day,
to have an answer to
yea or nay,
one turns to those of the way-
the only two that could play
and win this game
of yea or nay.

Was it really true
that amazons could be painted blue?
Was it really you
that stayed stuck together like glue?

"From here to death
and then beyond -
I'll never leave you."
is your response -
from one heart to another,
from one life t'nother.

Will you be
at the other side to greet me?
Will you be
by my side forever?

"Family we are now
and forever,
fates lived longer
and better together.

"Our paths were apart
until we met,
and then we traveled
through darkness
into the light.

"Time and time again,
we did battle;
alone - first you,
then me;
together - you with me.

"When two people merge
there is but one
life to live.
Through sorrow and joy,
happiness and pain,
all four seasons of living
at once.

Do you really love me
darkness and all?
Do you really love me for myself,
or just the ideal of love?

"I love your laughter
and I love your smile.
I love your innocence
and the inner light.

"Your love for me
and the world beyond
is what carries me through
the darkness that surrounds my past.

"So we continue on the path of life
living side by side,
loving life after life,
dreaming night after night."

Like the swirling waters,
the two lovers dance
in a graceful movement
that beckons our eyes
to follow our hearts.

Do you really care for me
and love me as a lover would?
Do you really see me
for all the questions within?

"Once I left you
for another,
with all the dreams
of being a wife and mother.

"Only to realize that
my life and yours
were no longer apart
but entwined
like the finest silks of Chin.

"You taught me
by your selfless giving
even when it caused
you unending pain.

"Your past is gone,
your sins forgotten
and freely forgiven.
Look towards the future
and once more, begin your
living.

"In all my questions,
you've answered many,
and those left
do not appear unending.

"Once more you step back
to allow free choice to
be my reign.

"For your love
chooses to be my guide,
to always have you
by my side."

My thanks for
questions answered,
neither coy nor
feeling pandered.

Through an age of love
and laughter,
do you have hope for
a life hereafter.

My questions given,
your answers sought,
to see whether lovers
you were or not.

In truth I see,
not just lovers
but more than mere friends
were meant to be.

To close this age
of rhyme and reason,
without mention
of heavy breathing...
if only to give cause
for us to believe in.

- title by TC/H

## 443. Expectations - 2001.02.23

When the expected never occurs,
the sound of disappointment
is shattering.

So you learn to expect less
and less
as time goes by
until the day comes
where nothing is expected
at all.

-title by KS

## 444. Nibble - 2001.02.25

The soft sweet sounds
of short sharp teeth
nibbling away
at the soft flesh.

Nip, nip,
nibble, nibble.

As small paws
maul white flesh,
a shout emerges
from somewhere far away -

-title by KS

## 445. Waiting - 2001.02.25

Waiting for the day to end,
waiting for the night to descend,
waiting with silent anticipation
for all the things that come out
under the cover of darkness.

Eyes wide open,
searching for hidden meanings,
looking beyond the words
for the feelings within.

-title by KS

## 446. Reminders - 2001.02.25

the bright summer sun
reminds me of your smile
even as the days
fade away
in a memory long gone.

the clear blue skies
bring back that day
so long ago
where all I can remember
are the golden tones
of your laughter

even as the days creep
towards the warmer months
ahead,
I look back towards
the time past for
that elusive
feeling
of anticipation...

-title by KS

## 447. 2001.03.01

There are few greater losses
to the heart
than that of
the unconditional love
that our friends would offer.

Even amongst the loneliest
of days,
never do our closest friends
forget us...
sensing our unhappiness,
sensing our loss.

They come up and hug you,
they pull you out to play -
even when your heart is not in...
they come over for comfort,
they remind you of the life
beyond today,
and into the future of tomorrow.

## 448. 2001.03.01

A heart once given can't return;
a secret once shared can't be
spurned.
Each day I lived became the past;
the hours you gave, I kept en
masse.

The distance between you and I,
grew greater as the time did fly.
My heart became ice cold,
t'another you were so bold.

Time forgets more than I
remember,
to forgive past hurts, stir the
embers.
Begin again, I must once more
try,
to trust again the look in your
eyes.

To mend a broken heart takes
time;
love ignores both reason and
rhyme.
Leaving the past where it
belongs;
looking forward to the hearts
song.

## 449. Heart's Thaw - 2001.03.02

A blanket of snow covers the
land,
as the traveler moves against
the swirling winds.

There is no search
for sheltering cover,
but for the forgiveness from
others.

Even as the footsteps trod
are covered with the snow,
our pasts are covered through
time.

As time moves on,
the sun emerges
to melt the unforgiving coldness
once more.

-title by EFM

## 450. Untitled - 2001.03.05

It might be the last heart you break
or the first time that you loved
that makes us live in the past.

Looking backward
even as we move forward
into a lifetime
beyond now.

Holding onto
the sweet memory
of the past
like the sensation that it was.

## 451. Untitled - 2001.03.06

For every answer given,
there's another question hidden.

Wandering around the fear,
against that is held dear.

Being alone is not the same,
for loneliness is a different game.

The past reflects the future,
but only if we allow it so.

## 452. Untitled - 2001.03.08

Are we looking for our answer
from without,
when we would do much better
searching from within?

What is truth
but an internal feeling
that tells us
what we can't ignore.

What is reality
but that which we see
and touch
and feel all around us.

## 453. A Touch of Silk - 2001.03.09

Ten thousand skeins of silk
scatter across skin
like a nervous dance
along the nerves.

The softest sound of laughter
skitters along the air
to reach waiting ears.

One moment in time
becomes frozen forever
in our memories
as the fading touch
leaves once more.

-title by TC

## 454. Winter's Fading - 2001.03.15

As the fading snowflakes
melt away under the sunshine,
a fresh scent of spring
arrives to greet us.

The clouds move
from dreary grey
to the white wisps
that remind us of our
own castles in the sky.

Very soon the sun will come
back
to greet us with a warmth
that we never forget.

-title by TC

## 455. Untitled - 2001.03.16

As harsh winter turns away
from the warmth of Spring,
the ice floes begin to thaw
once more,
running heedlessly
to the sea.

Spring thaw
bring with them
flash floods,
just waiting for that moment
where the coolness beyond the
ice
reflects the cold depths within.

## 456. Colossus - 2001.03.25

The glowing candles cast a
shimmer
throughout the evening,
as the shadows dance
against the white walls.

A splash of ouzo
sends the sizzling flame
jumping upwards,
a whirling frenzy
of liquid fire.

Time passes quickly
as the ebb and flow
of conversation
swirls around the room.

Too soon the merry company
parts
only to meet again
some day.

- title suggestions by Addicts;
- title by DB

## 457. Untitled - 2001.03.30

How do you mourn the loss
of someone you've always had?

How do you mourn the passing
of someone when you can't stop
the sorrow
that leaves you empty;
the sadness
that consumes you;
and hopelessness
that surrounds you.

When does loss leave you?
When does love stay the same?
When do you leave the sadness
behind
when you sift at the memories,
for they are all that you have left.

Time is the only thing that
passes quickly,
blurring our past as it fades,
it dulls the pain,
and bleeds away the sharp colors
that painted our lives.

## 458. 2001.04.04

The delicate balance between
here and not here
wavers every time
I stop and listen
for the words that are
inevitable -
harshly grating
on the nerves.

Like an unsightly blemish,
it is both blatant
and ignored at the same time.

I hear it,
but I don't hear it,
it's the same few words
that carve away
at the block of ice
that remains rigid
even at the height of summer.

The block is just a misnomer-
iceberg, or even, the barren
deserts
of the north,
where there are seven hundred
words for snow.

In the end,
the number of words don't
matter,
just the number of times they're
heard -
once more into the breach,
leaping across a chasm
that grows just a bit
further apart.

## 459. 2001.04.04

A depth charge is dropped
every once in a while,
exploding in the cold murkiness-
a silent rebound
into nothingness.

Every once in a while,
a bomb is thrown
into the middle of nowhere,
and all you feel
is the ground shaking.

Every once in a while,
I'm told that life is worth living,
but that too,
falls on deaf ears.

Every once in a while,
I remember to check myself,
to see, if I too,
am living.

## 460. 2001.04.04

Bitter laughter
finds no shelter in the sunshine.
It hides away
in the shadowed corners
of the dark.

Empty thoughts
have no response
unless you can hear
silent whispers falling.

Hollow eyes
reflect no joy
when you dream of emptiness
to fill the days.

Scornful lips
carry no weight
until you hear
the words again.

## 461. Untitled - 2001.04.05

Play the game,
play the game,
neither this team,
nor that team I bat.

Can't get to first base,
Never mind score the home
runs.

Am I playing shortstop,
or am I lost somewhere
in the outfield?

Play the game,
play the game,
sit back and watch them
run, slide,
hop, skip,
and dive, dive, dive
for the score.

## 462. Untitled - 2001.04.08

Bright sunshine and blustery
winds
highlight a Sunday morning.

For once, the quick and easy way
runs smoothly
from the center of the world
to points out west..

The mist of the falls
casts a fine rainbow
across the rocky shores.

Between a hard rock
as a musical place,
and the soft breezes
that blow across the bridge,
sunshine and smiles
are the order for the day.

Slipping and sliding
down the ice,
the cheering runs hot,
even as the temperatures
go cold.

Shoot!, shoot!, and awwws
run cross the rink
as the day ends
with no loss and only
happy memories.

## 463. Out of the Darkness - 2001.04.13

A day of atonement,
a day of passing
over those that were
forgiven once more.

A day of rebirth,
to place faith
once more
in humanity.

A day of darkness,
ungiving of light,
as our thoughts
linger once more.

-title by PS

## 464. Untitled - 2001.04.16

Like an endless torrent
of river flow,
the words echo silently
against the ice
that is the first barrier
against the deluge.

Every day, I remain watchful
of the rising levels
of power
the swift word
carries.

What I heard today
is the same
as the words yesterday.

There are only so many ways
to cut an inch of skin away -
one square at a time.

Just to remind you
that this is real,
rub some salt in please.

And the shock
reminds me that
this nightmare is real
that those words I did hear
were said deliberately
like a cannon through
a tissue -
the gaping hole left -
is disfigured and malformed
in the end.

I won't forget these words
spoken carelessly,
the wounds smart too much
for these hurts
to have been imagined.

I won't forget
the unending silence
you pretend to hear.

I left no words spoke,
I left no silences to be filled.

I left my soul behind
too many years ago
to truly care about
what you say
to an empty shell.

## 465. Untitled - 2001.04.16

Sometimes a cut
is just a cut,
to remind me
that I'm living.

Sometimes a tear
is all you hear,
to remind me
that I must be living.

Sometimes a sigh
is all you see,
a shrug
not worth noticing.

Sometimes my shadow
is all that is left
of the shell
that ever was.

## 466. Untitled - 2001.04.18

As the season progresses
we move from white to green,
from the snowy cold
that surrounds our winters
as we chase a black puck
across the ice;
to the gentle warmth
of a southern spring
where we chase a wee white ball
across the greens.

Summer greets us
in a flurry of black and white
kicked between footballers,
between two posts and a net.

As the leaves turn from green to gold,
once more we move to push
to gather baskets and shots
from the goal line...
as the nets move into the air
and everything is measured
in leaps and bounds.

## 467. Untitled - 2001.04.20

In and out,
in to the world,
out on the words.

Hidden past,
forbidding future.

The solitary road
beckons quietly
so that one
is out to the words
and in to the world.

No need to switch hit
or bat left or right,
no at bats to count
against you.

In and out,
a mask of a mask -
hiding all the layers
within.

## 468. Untitled - 2001.04.22

Day after day
night after night
hour after hour
the voice drones on
unending
and unrelenting -
a harsh grating
against my ears.

Close my eyes
and dream -
a day of silence -
golden solitude
and silvered shadows.

A day where
I heard myself
think,
speak,
and dream.

Instead of shrill calls,
shrieks
and screams.

One day where sunshine
could cast no shadow
where the rain drops
left no trace
of the meandering paths
they carved
against a hillside.

## 469. Untitled - 2001.04.22

What would you do on a day
like this
where all your dreams were
ludicrous
and no one could say I'm sorry,
no guts, no glory.

What would you do on a day
like this
where all year was her whine and
hiss
and no one could say go away
now,
not today, not now.

What would you do with a day
like now
the sun's out but you're
drowning some how.
There's no hurry
I'll tell you - don't worry.

What would you do with a child
like me
who doesn't act like a typical she,
there's no lurid story
I feel so hurried.

What would you do with a f*k
like me
where there's no shelter,
I don't scream "helter skelter"
there are no welts there.

## 470. Untitled - 2001.04.26

The silence I seek
is like a rainbow -
elusive in nature,
rich in colours -
but seldom had.

It's a bitter feeling
of emptiness
as the words echo
endlessly.

Bite your tongue
to linger on
in silence.

## 471. Untitled - 2001.04.26

I am drained of all joy,
and filled with dark dread.

I am empty of all thoughts,
a vessel of hollow smiles
and stolen dreams.

Just a pinprick
to remind me
of all that I loss.

Just a small scar
to remind me
of what I never had.

## 472. Untitled - 2001.04.27

I am weary
of all the things
that surround me.

The gilded cage
that reminds me
of the world
beyond here.

The bare sustenance
that means I will
see tomorrow
but maybe not next year.

## 473. 2001.05.03

Even as the door to one life
ends,
the windows of opportunity
opens
towards another.

The road winds up and down
even as we struggle
to find direction within
our own lives.

As the moon sets on one world.
already, the sun is rising
on new life.

It is never the beginning of the
end,
as it only marks the end of one
beginning,
and the start of another.

## 474. 2001.05.03

As I soar above the clouds,
I look past the grey and white
to see a beautiful clear blue sky
framed by the warm spring sun.

As we hurtle eastwards,
I imagine that I can see the
figures
white clouds make,
giving form to what
were only thoughts before.

## 475. 2001.05.03

There is a land above the skies
that is made up entirely
of white -
carving fjords and islands
out of the softest clouds.

Even as the sheep gambol
amongst the heathered greens
and sailboats cross the lakes
once more,
they drift away
from searching eyes.

## 476. 2001.05.03

As the sun moves across the land
in a blaze of glory,
it bathes the day in gold.

As it sets out to light the world,
it leaves an orange trail
amongst sky blue,
that makes us yearn for
tomorrow.

As darkness sets in for another
night,
we reflect under the moonlight
all that passed during the day.

## 477. 2001.05.04

Midnight comes and passes with
the silence of a creeping cat.

There is no mark that
echoes the fleeting image
of night crossing into day.

The single light seems lonely
in the doorway
as if waiting for its darkness
across the other side.

The low hum permeates the
room
as a casual knock
against the door
disturbs the silence
of the soft breathing
heard within.

## 478. 2001.05.04

The hours before dawn
are eerily silent
as the balance between
night and day
hangs upon a thread.

With the twist of a pin,
the faint whispers
of the early morning sun are
seen,
chasing away the last remnants
of the night just past.

As the cool morning air
is pushed by the warm breezes,
a pale pink is seen
from the edge of the world,
once more greeting the world
as the new day begins.

## 479. 2001.05.04

Mornings come early in May,
even as the faint mist
is burnt away
by the bright sunlight.

What begins as a cool dawn
quickly becomes a hot day
as the skies rapidly clear.

Through the city haze
we can see the distant specs
of the peaceful ocean,
the blue water broken
only by white waves.

## 480. 2001.05.04

-chocolate covered strawberries
with champagne

Fresh ripe red flesh
drizzled with
the sweetest of white chocolate -
a crisp shell on
soft core -
hardening against
pale pinkness.

## 481. 2001.05.04

-honeyed apples

Thinly sliced crisps
spread out across a sheet of
white -
with the lightest drizzle
of gold across the surface.

The slight tang of lemon juice
brings both a sweet and salty
taste to the tongue.

## 482. 2001.05.04

-raspberries + Grande Marnier

The red globes fall from above
onto a cloud of vanilla -
slipping off a metal slide into
pools of white.

A thin gold glaze of Grande
Marnier
changes the touch from rough to
smooth -
each sip leaves me
drunken and delirious
with the taste of desire.

## 483. 2001.05.04

-peaches and cream

Bright crisp halves
both juicy and smooth
are nestled in a
sea of white.

Smooth dabs of white
on the top
draw our eyes
to the tip
of the golden fruits.

Small nips
from the top,
combined with sharp nibbles
of the cream,
quickly reduces the mound -
disappearing in moments.

## 484. 2001.05.04

-Chocolate Mississippi Mud Pie

A bright red cherry
nestled in a sea of white cream
dimpled by flakes of chocolate.

A soft chocolate sauce
drizzled against the white,
sliding slowly into the nooks
of the cheesecake.

Rich, rich mud pie
melts in a slow,
succulent manner.

Each silent spoonful
drawing slow hums
of pleasure.

## 485. 2001.05.04

-strawberries and dark chocolate

The dimpled fruit
captures dark sweetness
in a simple motion -
being dipped up and down
in the steady stream of
liquid chocolate.

As it cools to the contact
of air on fruit,
it hardens to a sweet shell,
to be slowly consumed
bit by bit.

## 486. 2001.05.04

-melons + cheesecake + ice cream
+ almonds

Bright green, crisp orange
soft globes of sweet flesh,
split along the centre
and glazed with honey.

Each spoonful
cuts through smooth flesh
and soft cake -
the taste melts along
the tongue.

A light layer of almond slivers
adds a hard crunch
to soft cream.

## 487. 2001.05.04

-peaches + butter pecan ice
cream

On a plate of white,
the butter pecan melts
into a gentle pool
of pale cream.

The slivers of peach fruit
present a mellow contrast
to golden brown.

## 488. 2001.05.04

- grapes + honey

A melange of red, green and
black
globes spill across the glass,
glistening with a clear glaze
covering pale flesh.

Succulent spheres,
crisp centers,
endless rivulets
of honeyed grapes
drop onto a waiting tongue.

## 489. 2001.05.05

An early summer day
leads to a gathering by the pool,
eight different shades of pale -
sunglasses, and happy smiles
for the bright sunshine.

As the waves shift
within the pool,
the breeze
ruffles soft strands
under bright sunlight.

## 490. 2001.05.05

Every spoonful of cream
melts even before it reaches
a waiting mouth,
a drip falls uncaught
to the table,
pooling in a slight circle.

Running a finger up
and down the glass,
scraping the very bottom
of the shake,
until the spoon is clean...

## 491. 2001.05.05

- French apple crepes

A dusting of white powder
lands upon soft, pale skin -
almost translucent to the touch.

Tender fruits -
golden yellows,
delicious red centres.

Each nibble draws
a hum of pleasure,
each bite,
a sigh of release
as the deepening pangs
of hunger
are finally
assuaged.

## 492. 2001.05.05

- strawberry + dark chocolate

The blood red freshness
of strawberries
mingles with the sweet taste
of dark chocolate.

Each bite reveals
a pale pink center
mixed with the
succulent taste
of softened chocolate
mingling with the
lingering juices.

## 493. 2001.05.08

The early morning sun
glistens amongst the millions
of dew drops
that are scattered
on the many rose petals.

A garden of pinks and ivories
blooming on a hot spring day.
The luscious tranquility
echoes the trills of the songbirds
hidden amongst the bower
within.

## 494. 2001.05.08

The early morning calm
is broken only
by the crisp chirrups
of the birds outside.

A soft shadowed corner
provides a quiet sanctuary
and needed rest.

The sun moves from behind
trellised windows
into the garden
once more.

## 495. 2001.05.10

The early morning mist
envelopes the harbour
and its surrounding hills.

As the sun peeks beyond
the horizon,
it burns the mist
until it fades
into memory once more.

Sunlight casts
the brightly painted
houses into brilliant sheen.

## 496. 2001.05.11

I went to find my heart in San
Francisco,
to find my soul in the fabled
West.

I want to see the land of magic,
to live the life not found
in a treasure chest.

I want to see a thousand smiles,
and travel a million miles.

I saw the sights,
dreamt wild dreams
and laughed until it hurt.

## 497. 2001.05.13

The lush, fertile valley
bound by two mountain ranges
leaves me drunken
from verdant scenery.

As the hot warmth of the north
blazes down on globes and vines,
we are caught in the
emotion of the day.

A gentle breeze causes
the vines to sway
even as the sweltering sun
quickly dries up the small drops
of salty sweat
that would gather
at the cusp.

**498.** Ode to an empty Circle – 2001.05.13

To move quickly from a dull yellow,
falling into a liquid bath of hotness,
flopped over even before the side is golden.

The sizzle and hiss of a white glaze
that coats crisp gold flesh
remaining firm to the touch.

Each bite melts away
even as we struggle
to identify the taste.

A feast of tasty bits
dances before our eyes
as the myriad of selections
overwhelm us.

**499.** 2001.05.15

The ridges dance across
the golden flesh
even as the sun beats down
with growing strength.

The smooth curves are broken
only by the small indentations
akin to a dragons back.

**500.** 2001.05.15

The tingle of clear happiness
bubbles down the throat –
tickling the senses on the way.

A fruitful offering
on a crisp platter –
covered in hardened sweetness.

A small bite reveals red fruit,
pink depths and sweet juices
all mixing into a mélange of wonder.

A bit of chocolate,
the center of white meat,
and a sip of bubbly –
the opulent surroundings capture
our attention immediately.

**501.** 2001.05.15

A long look down a crooked street,
a trip across the harbour,
climb the hills to find a shrine,
find the pub, drink a pint.

From a city of angels
to that of Saint Francis,
the jaunt becomes an exploration
of places once fabled and fun.

Even as the sun rises on Cannery Row,
and the sea breezes blow in once more,
a brisk summoning to Pebble Beach,
then Salinas Valley is on the way.

## 502. 2001.05.16

The flat lands of Texas
are broken by the large patches
of green that dot the landscape.

The constant reminder of
the black gold
that fuels so much of "Yew-Stun"
lingers in the mind -
it permeates the very air
that we breathe in.

## 503. 2001.05.16

How often do you have a namesake
for a namesake?
From head to toe - all in black,
a strong, silent type eh? <g>

Choose, stuff, stitch, fluff,
dress, hear, name, then take me home.
I'm so easy aren't I?

Jr. cuts a swath through the room -
specs and all - a solemn look.
A combination of "no, no, no"
and then
"yes, yes, yes" from the other corner
I heard.

## 504. 2001.05.26

In the famed land of ten thousand lakes,
I saw a sea of green -
an endless wave of fluttering leaves
and quiet pines.

The true path to eternity
would see the winding roads
of Minnesota -
with the undying expanse of forests
that not only the harbor the insects,
but the plenitude of insects as well!

A weekend of fun,
passes all too quickly
as my travels end
three weeks of laughter.

## 505. Untitled - 2001.05.30

I'm looking for that silent place
within,
where I can't hear the voices
that wear away
on nerves long dead.

I'm searching for the silence
that is golden to my soul,
where all I can feel
is the heartbeat of another.

I'm finding that hidden nook
where the pain just fades away,
where the words wash aside
all the cuts made unknowingly.

I'm jumping into an abyss
of deathly emptiness,
where light does not enter
and hope does not escape.

I'm waiting for the end,
where the words will hold no
power,
and time will have no sway.

I'm hiding from the world,
knowing my knowledge is not
quite enough
to make the leap
from this life
to the next.

## 506. Untitled - 2001.05.30

All I really have left
are my memories
of happier days gone by.

All I really treasure
are those moments
of happy smiles and laughter.

All I really sought
was a moments respite
from the unrelenting wants
that rule me.

All I really need
is another moment
of peace.

## 507. Untitled - 2001.06.04

It is with the deftest of touches
that the eyes trace the light path
the honeyed glaze
carves along the strawberry nubs
that so command our attention.

Even as warmed honey
surrounds the chilled fruit,
the heat of the room
moves quickly out of control.

Each bite reveals
silken flesh
that beckons temptingly
for another taste.

## 508. 2001.06.07

A sip of hot liquid
whets the palate
just enough
to moisten the dryness within.

Each droplet
soothes parched lips
even as our eyes
drift away
to follow
the sweet scent
that wafts
from the neat squares
of pressed golden slices
holding
a confection of sweetness.

Each bite reveals
the tangy citron fruits
that linger on the edge.

A sip and a sup
elevates the art of slow
consumption ~
there is no hurry
the golden jelly
that holds toasted edges
together.

Every nibble,
every bite,
becomes audible
in the resounding silence
as the jellied sandwiches
become more than just
sustenance
and something closer
to food
for the soul.

## 509. 2001.06.09

The spongy crust
drinks up the honey glaze
like a thirsty desert
under a midday rainstorm.

Each spoonful
slips off the plate
onto a waiting tongue
pale gold lightness
against dark red flesh.

Short nibbles,
sharp sighs,
as each bite
disappears
under anxious eyes.

## 510. Pride Day - 2001.06.24

The bright sunshine outside
reflects the fervor
of the shifting crowds.

The roar of the afternoon
lifts a million voices
in cheers and laughter.

The rainbow flags are all aflutter
as the hot day shifts
to a night
of wild dancing.

## 511. Untitled - 2001.06.27

It is with the slightest push
that I watch
the pale green slice
slide along the edge
until
it
falls
onto
a
waiting tongue.

As the heat of the sight
warms the coolness within,
a steady pool of cream
gathers
and trickles
downwards
until
all
you
can
watch
is
that
single
droplet
of mint
chocolate chip
ice cream.

The sensation of icy coldness
within
does battle against
the searing heat outside
as the sweet delicacy
melts upon
your tongue.

## 512. 2001.07.01

The hot summer heat
is thick upon the air,
as the bright city lights
twinkle in the distance.

A lazy breeze ruffles
the weeping willows outside,
as the fan circles slowly,
moving dead air around the
room.

## 513. 2001.07.11

As the haze of clouds
move across the heavens,
a slow trail of white
is left lingering
against pale blue.

The single moment of silence
is broken by the roar
of engines against
fine gravel.

A rough wheel
spins helplessly
in the air.

## 514. Untitled - 2001.07.14

It's been a year -
a year since life
has turned upside down.

There is no real satisfaction
to winning this discussion.

Shame - is that all she feels?

Why is it really?

Reflecting on my failings?
her failings?

## 515. Untitled - 2001.07.14

It is with great irony
that almost a year to the date
of the first time...

There is no rest for the weary,
there is no rest for the wicked,
it is an unending struggle for
internal peace.

The moment
that I hear her voice -
it is a grating harshness
that booms.

An endless struggle for silence

An endless struggle for solitude
that protects me
from the torrent of words.

Who I am,
what I wear,
when will I die?

## 516. 2001.07.15

There is no silence for me,
another year has come and gone.

The loss of thirty is not enough,
another thirty is in order.

I'm sure that there will be one day
where I won't hear this.

I want one life, one day.

## 517. 2001.07.15

A million words,
ten million swords -
each nuance
gauging another chick
in the non-existent armour.

Every moment is
an eternity
as the venom
drips effortlessly
off her lips.

Every day is another sunrise,
a struggle against the world
without
even as I do battle within -
the demons that would castigate
have become like
baneful watchers
from within.

## 518. 2001.07.15

I gather
the hidden cloak
around me
where the worlds
slide off
like raindrops
against the windows.

So with this shroud
I walk once more
half dead
in the land
of the living.

Like a wraith
I slip
from shadow to shadow -
unbidden in the memories.

## 519. 2001.07.15

Like the torrential rains
of spring
the flood of pain
batters against
the crumbling banks.

There is nothing
that holds me here.

Nothing that ties me
to this life.

My clothing -
hath become that of the
collective.

My life -
exists to bend to the will -
of another,
and that is not me.

My existence
is but a flutter
in the sands of time.

## 520. Untitled -. 2001.07.15

Year after year,
time after time -
this is for your own good.

This is for your betterment.

The false concern
belies the true intent.

## 521. 2001.07.25

In this world
unfortunately,
there is never the assurance
that the footprints are ever
beside you
or even behind you
or if lucky, relatively in front of
you.

The laneways are narrow,
the alleys hidden
there is no reason for someone
to venture into the darkest
shadows
why smudge the clothing
when the walls are covered with
soot?

As it is,
it is easier to not mire someone
else
into the messes that would dot
the path.

## 522. 2001.07.26

Magic pen time -
curious how the
black ink flows
even when there is
no light.

There is only
the unending darkness
that subsumes
everything into
a gaping maw
of silence.

Even as the outside
quiets
until all you can hear
are the faint echoes
of laughter,
the rants
and raves
that mark this day
from the next
never stop.

## 523. Untitled - 2001.07.26

There is less and less
that holds me to this world.

Few things of value,
fewer bits to value.

Just for the sake
of morbid fascination,
I saw a railroad
today
seamlessly against
pale white -
and the quiet sound
of the thuds
left me wondering
that another ride
to
Never-Never Land
was not such
a bad idea.

## 524. 2001.07.26

Even as the breath
exits the body,
there is a cloak
of numbness
that descends
and muffles
the silent howls
left
unuttered.

Like rough leather worn -
it hides away
everything
that might have been
seen.

There is a slow measure -
as the pulse runs silently -
each moment
becoming
eternity.

Slowly at first,
until there is
a steady stream
of movement.

Isn't it ironic,
that the only thing felt
was the numbness
and then the pain.

I have forgotten
what
joy
is.

## 525. Untitled - 2001.07.26

She talks through the door,
I sit
in the corner.

What a conversation we have.

So here I am,
sitting in the dark,
armed with black ink,
black duster,
and black thoughts -
and the only thing
that grows -
is the tomorrow
that never comes.

## 526. Untitled - 2001.07.26

Pleasure -
what is it exactly?

Some ephemeral feeling
that never quite
satisfies
all the emptiness
within.

Pleasure -
that which is fleeting in time,
and nigh unforgettable.

Pleasure -
I take none
in this stolen life
I seem to be living.

Pleasure -
none to be found,
none to be had.

Pleasure -
a false illusion
that leaves me
wanting.

## 527. Untitled - 2001.08.01

Like the golden thread of
happiness,
her voice wends its way
across time and space
to wrap around
our heartstrings.

Tugging at emotions long
hidden,
and remembering memories
thought lost.
This bright strand of sunshine
brings hope unbidden.

Silvered tones of entreaty
echo against the silent shadows -
weaving the warp and woof
of our thoughts -
in her song.

## 528. Untitled - 2001.08.17

It's a gentle cascade of orange,
reds, and grape,
that falls across
the scoop of lime green and
white.

Summer bounty
crisply nestled against
a swirl of chocolate.

Drawing the wafers against
the edge
where light
and dark dance
a delicate path
between
absolute perfection
and
exquisite silence.

## 529. Untitled - 2001.08.17

Desolation draws a mark
across the page

There is very little left unsaid,
every last thought
is dragged from the grave,
like a reluctant guest
at a death bed gathering.

Months after things have passed,
they are thrown at you,
like a bucket of ice
to the face.

It's like the shameful events
that have come and gone -
pages fallen from a book
like a stain upon the pristine
white.

## 530. Untitled - 2001.08.17

My friends,
do not lament the loss
of what never was

Do not seek to remember
what is best
left forgotten -
like so much dust
to the winds

Eroding
and then falling
into the ocean
tides

## 531. Untitled - 2001.08.11/2001.08.17

The hot sun bakes slowly
until all that is left
are the shadows...

Dappled sunshine
against shadowed patios
until the water
washes words away

Gentle laughter
washes against the slight breeze,
even as dusk approaches
and light fades

Evening passes
into night, voices fading
until all that is left
are memories.

## 532. Untitled - 2001.09.08

In a moment of sweet clarity,
watch the droplets form
and then twist
in a meandering river
of succulent tastes
falls from the very edge
of your fingers
onto an outstretched tongue.

As the droplets gather
to become the pool
of lingering ambrosia,
the desperate attempts
to gather it once more
onto sweet lips and eyes.

A singular brush of gold
against the undulating flesh
winks pale
under the morning sunshine.

The sun casts
dappled shadows
across the whiteness
that fills the room.

A million sensations
dance across the nerves
as splayed limbs
and ragged breathing
are all that
is seen and heard.

Hushed whisperings
break the calm silence
as the last
of the lingering touches
leave only the trace
shadows of sensation.

## 533. 2001.09.17

In one moment of clarity,
there lies the shattering
of the dreams
of thousands
upon millions.

In one flicker of an eye,
I watched the world
turn upside down,
and then inside out.

In one unrelenting nightmare,
images are torn
from across a screen
looped endlessly,
even as the world
reeled from the horror.

In one hope,
we moved to help,
to find those lost,
reunite those separated
and mend the wounds
of the world.

With one voice,
we cried,
with each death,
we mourned,
until each moment
melded into the next.

But for one minute,
I would give,
to go back
but one week,
to find that sliver
of happiness

that cloaked our souls.

For one lifetime lived now,
struck numb by this terror,
wounded innocents no more.

One day at a time,
for all of those left,
as we move,
one step
after another,
forward.

## 534. Two - 2001.09.21

Two worlds in one day;
the before and after
of the shadowed cloud.

Two sides pit against
a middle -
vengeance, retribution,
and justice.

Two towers fallen,
a world mourns.

Even as we march towards the future,
two soldiers side-by-side,
forget not those that walked
before us,
carving this road
from war to peace.

Two wars have passed
through this world,
let not this be
the beginning of a third.

## 535. Untitled - 2001.09.21

A million raindrops fall
in rapid staccato against
the walkways
now abandoned.

The milky streetlights
scatter dim shadows
along sheltered doorways.

A distant splash of rain
against a gutter
is all the reminder
that there is a world
beyond the memories
surrounding this
one moment.

The cold droplets push
towards the edge of
the window
where hidden eyes
watch silently.

The swirl of warmth
from the fire
mixes with the cool
evening rain ~
leaving a somber evening
for the dreams
beyond this night.

## 536. Seven - 2001.09.25

Some say the world was made in
seven days,
but for so many,
their world crumbled two seven-
days ago.

Seven vices and seven virtues,
where does the line that
separates
"us" from "them" begin
or end?

The Bard spoke of seven Acts of
Man,
but we seem stagnant in the
fourth -
agitating for battle even as we
abandon peace.

This will be no seven-day war,
nor even a seven-week, nor
seven-month...
seven-year war as we struggle
to deal with terrors
from both without
and within.

## 537. Untitled - 2001.09.29

Pineapple explosions
fall from the heavens,
even as the prickly skin
breaks to see
a pale golden center
of tangy sweetness
that but mirrors
the one who tossed
the fruit over
in a careful lobbing
of a potential bomb -
that revealed itself
as an unexpected
dessert.

## 538. Untitled - 2001.10.03

Silence
meets flailing arms,
as words struggle to find a place
amongst the jumble of thoughts
that demand exposure
even as they fall over one
another
in the flurry to be heard.

A gaping hole forms in the room
where the burgeoning question
remains
like a pink elephant
amongst the furniture ~
sally forth or pull back,
where does each decision lead?

## 539. 2001.10.03

Silence
meets flailing arms,
as words struggle to find a place
amongst the jumble of thoughts
that demand exposure
even as they fall over one
another
in the flurry to be heard.

A gaping hole forms in the room
where the burgeoning question
remains
like a pink elephant
amongst the furniture ~
sally forth or pull back,
where does each decision lead?

## 540. Untitled - 2001.10.04

If yesterday was a quandary,
then today becomes a map
where all the paths move
beyond the point of now.

All of the tomorrows
are shifting,
blurring and bending away
from what was presumed
but a day ago.

Travelling without direction,
knowing only that it is
not here.

Direction mixed with distance,
either one at premium,
destination and journey
not always meeting.

## 541. 2001.10.04

If yesterday was a quandary,
then today becomes a map
where all the paths move
beyond the point of now.

All of the tomorrows
are shifting,
blurring and bending away
from what was presumed
but a day ago.

Traveling without direction,
knowing only that it is
not here.

Direction mixed with distance,
either one at premium,
destination and journey
not always meeting.

## 542. Untitled* - 2001.10.06

The bright moonlight
filters through the spiny limbs
casting misshaped shadows
on the floor.

A passing cloud
causes the light to dim
and flicker onwards once more.

A shaft of moonlight
reveals a hidden gem -
a small nub of sweetness
that beckons across the room.

Entranced,

my eyes trace
a delicate path
along sloping curves
topped by white.

Each slow suck
draws a river of liquid sweetness
that coats lips and tongue
in equal generosity.

Sharp nibbles
against a hardened surface
yields a soft core of sugar -
that sends me on a
euphoric high again.

The witching hour passes
and dawn finds me,
gathering the nubs
like hidden treasures -
all that is left to remind us -
of this bag of candy corn.

*Originally called the: Ode to
Candy Corn - as provided by Ms
Stephanie S :)

## 543. 2001.10.07

As the night darkens,
the full moon peeks out
from behind the gentle
wisps of clouds.

Lighting a path of silvery stars
on the night of Samhain,
the world takes on a
different glow,
as the veil separating
two worlds
shimmers
and then fades away.

As the young masquerade
in ghouls and goblins,
sharper eyes
catch the shadows
that gain form,
on the short night
that lies ahead.

A brief ceili
around a bonfire
quickly sends us away -
laughing out loud
at our fears given form.

Even as the jack-o-lanterns
saunter in the distance,
held by the headless Horseman
once more,
I remember the days
long past
where our fears
were like the will-o-wisps,
fading in the night.176

## 544. Untitled - 2001.10.07

The crisp moonlight
changes from milk white
to a pale orange
as the clouds part
to reveal
a round pumpkin
in the heavens.

I watch the flames
of the bonfire,
reflecting
in the glow of the eyes
that surround me ~
a gleeful glance
of those half-entranced,
reveal nothing more
to this night.

As the flickers jump
in a wild moondance,
I can see the edge
of the world between
now and forever
blur
until there is nothing
that separates us
in this delicate waltz.

Faster and faster,
the wind swirls until
the autumn leaves
dance amongst
the ghostly figures
that gathered around
us here.176

## 545. Untitled - 2001.10.08

A sprinkling of night frost
dust the tops of the pretty
punkins
sitting in a row.

Carved with faces both dark
and mirthful,
they are the greeters
of the ghouls
and goblins
at the door.

As the moonlight peeks
beyond the shadows of the trees,
the frost glistens silver,
even as the breaths of air
casts grey clouds in the night.

As the scattering of tea lights,
create a contrast of cool warmth
in the autumn nights,
all the gremlins
seek shelter amongst
the warm hearths
sipping at cups of hot cocoa.

Night gives way to dawn,
and the sinister faces
on wee punkins
fade away
to reveal
the jolly smiles
small hands did draw.

Transforming
once again,
only in the next moonlight.

- inspired by conversation with
Dame Judith

## 546. Untitled - 2001.10.10

The crisp jellybeans
of Halloween
are decorated in
bright orange and black.

Dropping small handfuls
along the main pathway
leading all the way
upstairs.

Hunting each one,
makes in part the fun,
find a few more
hidden away.

As I line them up,
curving along the edge,
they roll away
one by one
across a wide expanse
of paleness
that hides each jelly
once more.

As I neatly tuck them back,
each jelly is
a burst of excitement,
until all I have left,
are a few
lonely colours
quietly waiting
to fall in dark depths.

Slowly the last ones fall,
first orange, then black,
until the sweetness fades.

- inspired by conversation with
Miss Ellie

## 547. Untitled - 2001.10.15

As the sun sets,
the pool of liquid gold,
melds into rich darkness.

The moon rises
casting a pale glow
across pure sweetness ~
glistening in the starlight.

Each slow drizzle
across
crisp red surfaces
coats
firm skin
in pure
sensation.

Nibbling across
the cool coating
reveals
pale flesh
against
rich chocolate.

Each slow lick
parting
the surface
once more.

Biting
until
a core is found;
tasting
until all that is left,
are the pale seeds
for next time.

- caramel apples

## 548. Untitled - 2001.10.18

The path traced between two
points
converge in the middle
as we vacillate between
going left
or right.

The small jump
from one tip to the other
becomes forever
as the waiting
stretches
into the distance.

There is no real haste
in traversing the gap
from one to another ~
slowly meandering
across the expanse
of the plains.

The changing hip and valleys
of the landscape
beckon for closer examination
until all you can see
is thin line
where rough
becomes smooth.

## 549. Untitled - 2001.10.20

The late autumn gales
sound hollow
against the battered windows.

The colour grey is cast
against darkness -
like a shroud
of death upon the living.

Phantom fingers
draw themselves
against warm flesh,
raising goosebumps
on the way.

Each touch
like the faintest
whisper of sound
against pure silence.

Each breath
disappears
in the cool air.

Each gasp
falling
like the raindrops
just beyond
the world without.

A hush falls
as the starlight dims,

once more
I count the breaths
between each
and every
heartbeat.

## 550. Untitled - 2001.10.23

It's the bittersweet taste
of chocolate
that captures the attention.

What starts out as sweet,
wavers between ecstasy and
agony - even as each lick
diminishes all that is left.

Saving the best for the end -
the happy sweetness
of the last bite
is followed by the
disappointment
of nothing more.

A desperate search
reveals no more dessert for a
time...
until all across the land,
lanterns are lit,
and goblins flit
between door to door
asking for treats
from street to street.

A quick scramble
to find more sweets,
then giving them away,
suddenly all that's left
is a wee punkin
and a plate of chocolates.

As the orange light dims,
all thoughts turn inwards,
leaving the disguises outside,
the sweetness melts away
in the gentle October fire.

## 551. Untitled - 2001.10.25

It's a delicate balance
upon a blade,
sharing fire and ice
at the same time.

Fiery drops of heat
are quickly followed
by a gently cold kiss -
freezing fire
in its brilliant form.

Molten shadows meld,
and then blend
with the icy tendrils -
forming pools
of liquid warmth.

The candle light plays
against a million shadows -
each forming and reforming
once more.

Peeling away the disguises
that are donned every day,
the merest of flesh
and bone -
until all that is left
are the feelings
that run hot
and then cold.

The cool evening breeze
plays against heated flesh
until the thoughts
melt into nothingness
and reform once more.

## 552. Untitled - 2001.10.26

Each ridge is perfectly even,
bending towards a circular
middle,
the contrast of smooth outside
with the rough inside
is forgotten
with each nibble.

Until all that is left,
are the crumbs
stuck to the fingers -
swirling wet tongue
against sticky fingers -
the small cups
are left to be
forgotten at one side.

The light buttery paste
becomes a delectable spread
across a surface
first silken,
then roughened
as it is captured
by hidden crevasses.

Can't ever have just one -
a pair of perfect round bites
begin to melt against
the warm surface...
where it leaves a sweet
sticky print.

A crumpled bag of small
black cups is the only remnant
of the rich chocolate crust
that covered peanut butter.

- inspired by a PBC mention
from Missy Good

## 553. Untitled - 2001.10.28

It is the slightest touch
of the feather,
drawn along the edge
that creates
the sweetest sensation heard.

For countless moments,
all that is felt,
is the slowing heartbeat
against the silence of the room -
waiting for the next flicker
of that white down.

Each gentle sweep
across warm flesh
leaves expectations hanging.

Each touch is mirrored
by the tightening grasp
of nails
against pillowed down.

This faint pattern
of hide and seek
continues -
easing, then releasing,
until all that is seen,
is the tense bow drawn -
the entire body arching -
for that elusive touch.

Like an indolent cat,
basking in the hot
summer afternoons,
this cool autumn morning
finds the pool of intense warmth
to be the perfect reason
to stay inside once more.

## 554. Untitled - 2001.10.29

The late fall season
sees the rapid change
in Nature's colours
as the weather begins to cool.

A bright Sunday morning
greets a flurry of packing
as summer toys are stored away.

The partly strung
tennis racquet recalls
the hot summer afternoons,
where the susurrant sound
of a swinging arm
was the calm contrast
to the hard "thwack"
against the ball.

Swinging it one more time,
it lands in a box,
destined for the basement
corners.

- based on words provided by
Dee R - racquet; susurrant;
basement

## 555. Untitled - 2001.10.30

The golden tones
of a tune long lost -
remind us of the singer
gone before her time.

From smooth velvet
to rough silk,
the dulcet harmony
is what lingers in our hearts.

Every time we listen
and feel that silvered voice
once more,
we are transported
on a cloud of nostalgia
to that day,
where we sat
front row center
in her life.

- based on words provided by
Judith - singer; transported; front
row center

## 556. Untitled - 2001.10.31

The cool October night
harkens back to the summer past
-
where we sought
the cool ocean breezes
against the oppressive heat.

Another trip to the beach
lets us sit under the umbrella
shades,
sipping on cool tangerine juice -
its sticky sweetness
transporting us away
from the shrill cries
of the seagulls.

As dusk falls,
I watch the rotating beam
from the lighthouse
flash across
the turbulent waters of the
Atlantic,
mild gusts were the only succor
against that balmy summer day.

- based on words provided by
Miss Ellie - tangerine; lighthouse;
balmy

## 557. Untitled - 2001.11.03

Every kiss
is sweeter than all that is -
like the first sun ray
in the morning,
or the last moonbeam
of the night,
each touch
is lighter than before.

Every moment
becomes a story told
over a thousand and one nights;
each day
becomes an endless dream
that feels almost real;
each lifetime
passing in but a blink of the eye.

Carried on the late autumn
breezes
are the whispers
of words from far away -
even as
the leaves are swept
in the November winds,
thoughts become words,
and words become real.

## 558. Untitled - 2001.11.03

A flurry of November snow
leaves a blanket of white
outside.

The snapping fire
gives warmth to the room
even as
the sips of hot Mocha
form a lulling counterpoint.

A slow afternoon passes,
watching the snowflakes fall.

The mild harmony of TC
crooning her songs soothes,
until the cocoon
on the couch
becomes the shelter
against the cold outside.

- based on words provided by
DM - Mocha Cappuccino, Terri
Clark, and couch

## 559. Yesterday's Past - 2001.11.05

In the chilly shadows
of the November moon;
I am reminded that all things
come due on promises made.

A howling whistle
runs through the forest,
rattling the leaves
along the way.

Every crunch against
lifeless leaves
reverberates through the night.

Darkness casts a pale shadow
on the forest floor -
weaving life and death
in and out.

A growing hunger
in the night -
for warmth and shelter
drives the footsteps
faster -
until we lurch
into the welcoming circle
of light
at the end of this day's path.

## 560. 2001.11.05

Every day is like a comic book
reading,
where we all fall forward
into a world of true belief.

Every time, we begin
a new adventure
where all we feel -
is exhilarating.

A real life Alice in Wonderland
transforming the mundane
into the dream of a place
called Pup Island.

- based on words provided by CS
- comic book, exhilarating, Pup Island

## 561. Untitled - 2001.11.10

Hanging by the moment,
where release is but the letting go,
and safety
is nowhere to be found.

Every second
becomes a desperate search
for another nook and cranny,
stretched
out on a limb,
fingers taut with tension,
until it all becomes frail.

A simple unfurling
becomes a free fall...

## 562. Untitled - 2001.11.11

The first snowflakes
fell this evening -
white against
the silvered limbs of naked trees.

A gentle dusting
of white against the window
ledges
formed and melts away
even as the next flakes
gather courage to land
once more.

As night deepens,
the dark becomes light
as the shadows are filled
by this layer of softness
that disappears in the morning
sun.

# 563. 2001.11.10/2001.11.14

Indentations - first indentations
are by CS
Second indentations are by TJR

Hanging by the moment,
where release is but the letting
go,
and safety
is nowhere to be found.

Every second
becomes a desperate search
for another nook and cranny,
stretched
out on a limb,
fingers taut with tension,
until it all becomes frail.

A simple unfurling
becomes a free fall...

    like a tear
    slowly winding down
    a saddened cheek.

    A ring and a sigh
    a sound for all to hear
    like a whisper on the wind
    a message is sent.

    Hearts soar to
    the mountain and
    a white light
    shows the way.

    A plume of smoke rises
    and dust settles . . .

to permit Angels to
claim their charges
and show them the joys
of renewed life.

    So Guardian Angels are born

    to protect fellow hero's
    in their plight to save lives,
    in a world so filled with
    uncertainty and fright.

Sifting through the fiery ashes,
we struggle to find hope
within despair.

Digging deeper into darkness,
we search for unending light.
Looking beyond the surface
into the myriad of emotions
that colour everything we do.

## 564. 2001.11.18

The music reverberates
through the spine
as the whoops of laughter
echo beyond the brightly lit
room.

A frenzy of dancing surrounds
the evening of laughter
and cheer.

There is very little
to restrain the unending
enthusiasm.

The music of the seventies
speed into the future
as a flurry of bass beats
overwhelms the neighbourhood.

Dancing queens
and drag kings
make their appearance
at this royal gala.

## 565. 2001.11.24

Sipping on that first
Cafe con Leche,
we are reminded
of the rich depth
inherent to the cup.

Rich, dark, sweet
with just a hint of fire -
it warms the heart
from the very first moment.

From the very first taste
in Miami,
it becomes an affair of the heart,
to love her
means appreciating
every nuance
that is revealed
over time.

- based on words provided by
TJR- Cafe con leche, to love her,
Miami

## 566. 2001.11.25

In the lush Southern clime,
where the days pass by so slowly,
there is a sense of impending
excitement -
it is the vague line between
expectant joy
and unknowing fear
that greets every hurricane.

The furious torrent of rain drops
chases us back from Key West,
matching the thunderous
applause
for three Diva's
who let none leave disappointed.

- based on words provided by JE -
hurricane, Key West,
disappointed

## 567. Untitled - 2001.11.25

The first snow falls in November
casting a pale dusting
against the frosted windows.

As the late afternoon fades away,
the warmth of the fireplace
beckons
and sips of hot cocoa
heat us from inside out.

The setting sun
crosses the evening horizon,
changing from dark orange
to a shade of pale cherry.

The night sets in
against the haze of warmth -
watching the snow fall
on the pines beyond.

- based on words provided by VS -
snow, cherry, sunsetting

## 568. Untitled - 2001.11.29

Like a whimsical dream
of lollipops and unicorns,
our thoughts drift into
the joyous memories
of times before.

A dizzying ride
on the merry-go-round
in Central Park -
a green oasis
in a jungle of urban living.

We are drawn back
to our childhood days
where we played
knights and queens -
silvery hairnets
serving as both
veil and armour.

- based on words provided by
DR ~ joyous, Merry-Go-Round
in Central Park, NYC, hairnet

## 569. 2001.12.02

I thought I fought a coup d'etat
half-hearted at best,
if at that.

Not knowing the reasons I went
to fight,
a battle began, with no end in
sight.
I travelled afar
from my native home,
like the cowboys of old -
across the arid range, I roam.

Contrasting ideas fought out in
real life,
loss mirrored in unending strife,
each side cast in black and white,
ignoring all the shades of grey
that lay between then and now.

- based on "I thought I fought a
coup d'etat" from BM

## 570. Untitled - 2001.12.02

One thin second separates
the moment between two lives
meeting, and then departing.

Two words become the guiding
light -
"before" and "after"
the crossing of two lives.

Three tenets in staying together -
faith, hope, and charity -
with giving and receiving of the
same.

Four corners to which we scatter,
the distance is never too far
from our hearts.

Five reasons on each hand
to reach for pen and paper,
communication over land.

Six degrees of separation
from the connection
between near and far.

Seven colours in the rainbow
brings the luck we all need,
until we forget that Lady Luck
pays us no heed.

Eight-fold path to peace within
is balanced by
the multiple facets mirrored
without.

Nine lives for a cat,
living each moment
to the fullest of its days.

Ten is the number counted
on both hands - the time that
separates
perfection from life as it is.

## 571. Untitled - 2001.12.05

In a city of power,
there lays only a field of ashes,
that serve as the living reminder
of the loss that swept through
one day.

In a land where the north wind
blows,
a blanket of white snow
falls against the darkness of the
night ahead.

Under the miasma of lethargic
remembrance,
we seek the blissful peace
once found
in oblivion.

- based on words provided by TS
- field, blissful, peace

## 572. Untitled - 2001.12.07

Like the feel of silk sheets
against soft skin,
the words slide against each
other
in blind patterns
that leave us breathless
in this sensuous moment.

It becomes the first time
sunlight touches pale skin;
or the last drop of sweat
against the junction
of neck and shoulders.

Like the first snowflake
landing on a warm window pane
-
the perfect form
melts quickly
into a pool of clarity.

~ Based upon the WOTD by
Dame Judith ~ Sensuous

## 573. Untitled - 2001.12.08

Like golden honey flowing
off of red rose lips,
the gentle sweetness
takes the sting out
of the acerbic tang
of winter fruits.

The gamut of tastes
run roughshod over
the senses -
a gradual cascading
that increases in intensity
with every moment.

## 574. Untitled - 2001.12.15

The soft snow
casts a silvered silhouette
against the naked limbs
bathed in the moonlit darkness.

The absolute silence is eerie
as the midnight hush
falls upon the world
sleeping.

Dawn sees the edges of sunlight

peeking beyond the horizon -
lighting the crystalline icicles
in a rainbow of colours.

## 575. Untitled - December 15, 2001

In a flurry of whimsy,
the most innocent of phrases
becomes the launch station
for a list of Pups.

A rapid cascade of quips
that "go there"
faster than the express bus
filled with pups and leather
couches.

At the drop of a word,
going there becomes the exercise
of the day.

At the slyest of glances,
words becomes the way we play.

- based on words provided by ST
- pups, going, bus

## 576. Untitled - 2001.12.15

As the steam fogs up
from the hot bath tub,
it curls around the mirror
in the gilt picture frame.

My eyes wander from
the froth of white
through the mist
that dulls the senses.

As the gentle waves of warmth
wash against the edge
of white porcelain,
resting against the soft pillow,
I regain the serenity
that sustained me.

- based on words provided by
DR - picture frame; sustained;
bathtub

## 577. Evening Song - 2001.12.17

Every night
the world is undone
winding out in a ribbon of inky
darkness.

In the pale moonbeams
a forest of limbs
dances a ghostly turn,
shimmering with the snowflakes
from the morn.

A silver ribbon
runs through the path,
sparkling under the
chiaroscuro of earth
and water.

The last of the white lilies
float along with our eyes
as we wend our way
through the subtle
pleasures of light and dark,
hard and soft,
here and there.

The floating lights on
the rivers edge beckons
to the traveler to chance
a crossing against rough waters.

## 578. Untitled - 2001.12.21

The shortest day,
the longest night,
from dusk to dawn
the darkness lasts.

As the sun sets
beyond the hills,
the small flickers
of candlelight begin.

Warding against the pitch black
that would consume all light,
bonfire gatherings,
and happy times
are relived this night.

As the land begins its shift
around the sun,
the world moves
to embrace the warmth
from a million hearts.

## 579. Succulence - 2001.12.22

Even the scent is intoxicating
as the fleshy fruit
changes from deep, dark red
to a pale clarity.

Engorged in pure sweetness,
each bite makes us dance
in a drunken stupor.

Sucking slowly
to draw all the nectar
from the center –
I wonder
how these cherries
would taste
cast in chocolate.

- name provided by WC

## 580. Untitled - 2001.12.24

The feel of cool leather
sliding on warm flesh
is a tantalizing glimpse
at the senses.

Each nip and tuck
of the rough leather
against smooth silk
reveals a secret pleasure.

Like a shadow figure
in the dreams,
the first touch
transcends all imagination.

First night, last light,
hidden eyes meet
and then glance away
at the last sprig
of mistletoe.

- based on words provided by KS
- mistletoe; transcend; secret; leather

## 581. Untitled - 2001.12.26

Under the bright city lights,
there is a soft layer of white snow
landing against the many
window panes

Soft puffs of warm breath
cast magical figures
against the frosted glass.

The inside chill is banished
by the gentle roar
of the scent of cedar
burning
against fresh pine.

Soft jazz and endless
conversation
provides counterpoint
to the flurry of snowflakes
outside.

## 582. Untitled - 2001.12.27

The words travel across a glass
bridge
of a thousand miles
forming a pleasant distraction
from the monotone evening.

Each word becomes another line
in the image
that is drawn
from the imagination.

Even after all the echoes fade
with the dimming of the evening
light,
the words remain in the annals
of time
until reality replaces memory
once more.

## 583. Untitled - 2001.12.29

On a cold winter's day
with snowflakes outside,
three cats lay
against the warmth
of the cushions
upon the floor.

Tugging away
at a ball of string,
they hide underneath
the shy glances
all around.

As the skein unravels,
they chase the ends
all the way upstairs.

- based on words provided by
WC - ball of string, underneath,
upstairs

## 584. Untitled - 2001.12.29

In the crisp winter air,
the joyful barks of Dixie
chasing the snowflakes
falling along the beach
area a sycophantic echo
to the crash of the lake waters
against the shore.

The smallish shadow
becomes the reality
of Wing, bundled
from head to toe
in mufflers and hats.

At the flickering blinks of white,
there is a silent battle
being waged on the sandy front -
Dixie ends the jousting
for dominance in the cold
by running back
to the warmth that is home.

- based on words provided by DB
- Wing, snow, Dixie, beach, jousting

## 585. Untitled - 2001.12.02

In the early hours of the morn,
when the warmth still cocoons
the world,
there is a silence that fills the
room,
like a favourite blanket from
yesteryear.

A gradual shift
from slumber to wakefulness
begins with the faintest of
whispers
in the air.

Each moment of minute
pleasure
slides into the next,
until it becomes
a literal cascade of heat
against the still cool
outside.

Once more,
the morning silence is broken
by a single gasp
of pleasure/pain
hanging heavy
in the air.

## 586. Untitled - 2001.12.31

With a flash of a smile,
time stops for that moment
as the cold breath hangs
in between two worlds.

The very next moment
sees the hearts again beating
once more
in the rhythm of time.

In a blink of an eye,
the mind turns from the now
and here
towards the vague unknown
that is the future.

A fey smile
completes the image
of the not-reality
that caught my eye.

## 587. Untitled - 2001.12.31

As the frozen waves
crash against the icy shore,
the ducks waver
into the ebbing tide
until they float away
into the oncoming darkness.

the pebbles on the beach
are rough to the touch,
the crackle of the winter leaves
loud in the silence of the
walkways.

As night approaches,
the shadows enveloped
all the passersby.

## 588. 2002.01.01

On the last night of the year,
there are many beginnings
to carry forward into the future.

First night, last sight,
first touch, last light,
that forms the bridge
between now and then.

Fingers, slide and lock
into a solid grasp
tugging at invisible (heart)strings.

In the opening minutes
of the new year,
there are already
hints for a future -
where first and last
are circular.

## 589. Untitled - 2002.01.02

Pale hands that are cool to the touch,
are wrapped in the warmth of velvet green,
but even with the heat of the inside,
long fingers remain
like fresh snow upon white birch.

A single clasp of warmth against cold
begins the challenge
of finding a medium
between fire and ice
without the loss of contact.

## 590. Untitled - 2002.01.03

twitterpated
is the word
that matches
the feeling of falling...
down the stairs
in a hazy moment
where the floor/truth
rushes up to meet
the head and body
in one fell swoop
leaving me addlepated

## 591. Untitled - 2002.01.04

The pitcher of water
disperses the faint glow
of the mis-shaped candle
across the expanse of the room.

It casts a faint "X"
upon the wall
as the last flicker of the city lights
bounce against the windows.

- based on words provided by W. Chan - water; glow; X

## 592. Untitled - 2002.01.05

T'is the gift of dreams and possibilities
that remains the most significant
of the season.
Immeasurable is the knowledge
that joy might be hidden
around the next corner.

Of words, there may never be many,
but the thoughts and actions inherent
speak much easier
than those of the heart, mind and soul.

Like a beam of sunshine
across a dark hinterland,
everything is truly changed
even though they appear
the same.

## 593. Untitled - 2002.01.05

It is the bittersweet knowledge of parting
that makes each meeting beyond price.

Turning like the inevitable tide
in the race against time,
each moment stretches out
into countless minutes
and endless hours.

Time becomes something
beyond the ken of humans
when it passes at great speed.

Until the very last moment
between two times and
everything melds together.

## 594. Untitled - 2002.01.06

As silence descends upon the room,
it takes on a new shape -
no longer the emptiness
it was for so long.

It metamorphosizes
from a cool sense of observation
to a warmer sensation of patient anticipation.

Every quiet place within
is no longer pain-filled
as it was for long.

## 595. Untitled - 2002.01.06

There is a subtle shift
in all things
as the title changes
from the outside observer
to something very different.

All the thoughts previous
fell upon the page like
so many raindrops from the sky.
But that was just watching others
and asking the rhetorical -
what is real? what is not?

The unknown toppled under
the suddenness of reality,
truth shattering the fear
always held.

## 596. Untitled - 2002.01.06

Poker faces
against the world
even as the hand dealt
holds so many kings and queens
that any princely change in sums
would have revealed
what Lady Luck so kindly gave.

Even as fingers clasp together,
no attention is drawn
to the subtle shift
of satisfaction settling with the
eyes -
solid in the knowledge
of a winning hand.

In a silent nod to convention,
I'll carry the hand to the very
end,
all eyes forward,
learning to keep my poker face
on.


## 597. Untitled - 2002.01.06

Time does not count
in days, hours, and minutes...
it finds itself
in the long moments of silence
shared;
it finds itself
in the days that pass by so
quickly -
as happy we are,
in just being there.

Time becomes the endless
moments
of speechlessness that followed...


## 598. Untitled - 2002.01.06

The last voice I heard at night,
the first thought in the morning
~
both things are the same,
where four words become a
linchpin
for all else.

Even as we meet,
the knowledge of the parting
lurks,
so with sudden realization ~
"I miss you, already."
becomes the truth as we know it.

Like a rollercoaster,
the heartrending thrills
of the wild ride
between fright
and joy
beckons at the same time.

## 599. Untitled - 2002.01.06

Where does reality become
fiction
and the truth become like lies?
Where does conversation stop
and speculation begin?

Does the truth become stranger
than fiction?
Does fiction lead to truth?
What happens when truth
becomes embellished
to be a mockery of itself?

What's the shifting line
between too much and nothing
at all?
When happens when it does
stop ?
Like a merry-go-round
it spins itself into a tizzy
just trying to separate
truth from fiction.

## 600. Untitled - 2002.01.07

If forever was something that I
couldn't even envision
then I'd believe in tomorrow-
a length of tomorrows
that might lead to forever.

Not willing to portend the
vagaries of forever
but placing my faith from one
day to the next.

## 601. Untitled - 2002.01.07

Every memory becomes a pearl
on this string of large white
beads -
interspersed by the diamond
sharp images
captured in the mind's eye.

In times of silence, these jeweled
lengths come out,
the slow "clack" leading us to
remember the times...
counting away the days
until the next time
when more memories are made.

Hard pearls, sharp diamonds ~
they form the links
that draw us both together.

## 602. 2002.01.08

In the heart of winter,
the snowflakes fall fast and
furious,
creating a silent panorama,
even as the warmth
curls around us.

The pure whiteness against
the dark night sky
is silent
even as I am listening
for the breaths against
the cold air.

I remain captivated
by the flurry of crystalline tears
falling from the heavens...
until I realize that they are
but a reflection of within.

## 603. Untitled - 2002.01.09

A handful of
light and dark starfish
stare back
from the depths
of dark chocolate-y brown.

As each white/raspberry star
nestles in the centre of cool
palms,
the warmth of the remembrance
seeps back into the moment.

## 604. Untitled - 2002.01.09

The harsh cold wind brushes
against the fuzzy scarf,
searching for every nook and
cranny.

In the soft morning light
filtered through the grey skies,
the flutter of seagulls
can be heard against the crash
of the small waves.

Sliding across frozen ice,
the fear and exhilaration
do battle with
the sensation of giddiness -
all three vying
for a moment of sunlight.

## 605. Untitled - 2002.01.09

Every smile
seeps into the memory
like a gradual pool of sunlight.

They tug at the heartstrings,
open and happy to be here.

Silence becomes a treasure
as each moment shared
becomes a memory that
is stored into infinity.

Knowledge sinks in
like heavy cream
filtering through
all the depths
of the self,
even as the knots of worry
untie themselves
in a flurry of words.

## 606. Untitled - 2002.01.10

I would hope to
fly me to the moon,
to catch a moonbeam in my hand,
to play amongst the stars
'til the sun rose across the land.

I would surround the gossamer moonlight
in a basket of pure silver -
then wait for burnishing sun/gold
of the morning rays
to cradle each other;
as does the day would to the night.

Each bright smile
liquefies to a spot of warmth
that covers this silver/gold basket
of happiness.

## 607. Untitled - 2002.01.11

In the early morning hours
even before the sun rises,
a blanket of silence
lies heavy in the air.

Even as the stars blink away
from the daytime eyes,
thoughts leave and turn towards
wondering if everyone sees the same
constellations
with the clarity
of this not-yet daytime.

On and on,
the stars tumble across the heavens
until they too,
find their place
amongst everything else
that brightly shines.

## 608. Untitled - 2002.01.11

It is falling through a million
layers
of white haze and clouds
until you realize
that landing means
a stop to everything
that is happening.

For an endless moment,
there is a wavering
as to whether ending
this freefall
is even possible,
until you discover,
that already,
heartbeats,
thoughts,
and directions
became synchronous
in the first minute
of meeting.

This continuous flight
becomes a silver clarion call
as the idea
becomes reality.

## 609. Untitled - 2002.01.11

Even though the song says
that a kiss is just a kiss
and a sigh is just a sigh
what is a song
but a dance of words
and music together
in perfect harmony.

It becomes one single moment
of beauty and perfection
all swirled into
an endless time
of here.

The wonder of anticipation
and then realization
causes spirits to soar
even as hearts plummet
in an unending cascade
of sensation.

Boundless joy
meets reality
and life is forever changed.

As time goes by,
the answers will reveal
themselves
as to whether
this was the beginning
of a lovesong.

## 610. Untitled - 2002.01.12

The maelstrom of thoughts
swirl endlessly
in a mass
of anxiousness and anticipation.

As the roiling feelings
settle in the mind,
once more
the worries sink
into the murky depths
of the past.

## 611. Untitled - 2002.01.12

Like a moment of instant
chemistry,
Avogadro's number* is not
sufficient
to describe all the different
thoughts
that jostle for dominance
in the mind.

As time passes -
some combination of fast yet
slow,
the memories embed
themselves into the minds eye
with crystal clear precision.

Every word is like a strum
across the chords of the mind -
playing in perfect harmony
the echoes of a time past
and harbinger
of a future found.

*Avogadro's number is
$6.0221367 \times 10^{23}$

## 612. Untitled - 2002.01.12

Title - Lone Star Sinners (The
Hottest Action in the Hottest
State)

In the Lone Star state,
watching the tumbleweeds roll
in the distance,
the midday sun
beats down on the hard earth
with unrelenting heat.

Even the shadows seek shelter
in the hottest state of the land.

A subtle shift
brings attention
to the languid movement
of a tanned face -
each drop of sweat
neatly framed
between hazy eyes.

The flicker
of sunlight
catches the rough tip
of a pink tongue
against the surface
as it rasps smooth whiteness
into a swirl of sensation.

One slow continuous lick
from tip to top
ends in a slow smile
of satisfaction...

As the activity
increases at a frenzied pace,
the dribbling

down the chin
pool once more
somewhere beyond
the edge of the shirt...

Sharp nips along the collar bone
catch every drop
of
cold
ice cream
that has slowly
found its way
across
fingers,
tongue,
and
finally
parched flesh.

# 613. Untitled - 2002.01.14

-Hell on High Heels (She's got 8"
stilettos  and she isn't afraid to
use them!)

In the early morning hours
the almost silent shift
of a tight leather mini
is nearly missed
with an inaudible sigh.

Heads turn
to watch
the statuesque
walk,
and marvel
at the careful balance
between the terror
of falling
and the confidence of knowing

she won't.

It's the subtle swish of
hide against
the fishnets
that ratchets
the tension of the moment -
so minute,
it becomes ingrained
deeply
into the psyche.

Every step
becomes a moment
forever remembered
as eyes travel
from the rough stone edges,
wandering left,
then right...
high heels never slipping
on the uneven ground.

The curve of the ankle
is where I linger -
transfixed
by the simple
beauty of the moment
inches away from the ground.

Slowly,
the gaze shifts
ever upwards -
gliding past
smooth calves,
to strong thighs -
all lovingly wrapped
in the softest
of dark silks.

An inner purr begins,

as the vision becomes clear -
sleek curves
and strength --
barely restrained
in a shiny
new jacket.

As the day peeks
over the horizon,
the sunlight plays
across black shades,
and reflects from
the bright chrome
that surrounds us.

Even as I let go on the throttle,
and ease onto harsh pavement,
I can feel both arms
and thighs
tightening
around me -
carefully shifting
the rider (and bike)
into a higher gear
even as we ride
into the sunrise.

## 614. Untitled - 2002.01.14

As the night sky darkens
and the snowflakes fall,
the mind drifts along
with no worries.

Elastic in breadth,
the memories move forward
in our thoughts -
moments endless in
remembering details
from times gone by.

A tender smile is all that is left
against everything else that
happened -
framing one moment in
absolute clarity.

Etched by blade
against granite stone,
these few words
serve their purpose -
encapsulating
everything felt
in my mind.

## 615. Untitled - 2002.01.14

Every day was a gift -
everything felt - intangible.

Memories could not compare
to the reality that was.

Priceless was every moment -
living each minute beyond just
sixty seconds -
each time eyes met -
it became the highlight
of the day.

In a swirl of emotions -
the line between
what was real
and imaginary
blurred
until everything
became a flight of fancy.

## 616. Untitled - 2002.01.15

As the sea of snowflakes
fall in unrelenting flurry,
memories swirl back to
the surface of today
from the annals
of yesterday.

Unspoken words entwine
themselves
in the silent gestures
that form part of forever.

The quietude and silence
nourishes a need
just to be close.

The snowflakes melt slowly
and trace the tracks
all the way down
the windows.

## 617. Untitled - 2002.01.16

The crunch of boots against
fresh snow
is loud against the silence
of this winter evening.

Small puffs of air
breathed into the cold frost
hang for just a moment
against the dark sky.

Even as the skin is chilled,
the soul is warmed
by the comforting knowledge
that this walk on a winters eve
is shared
and not alone.

The ever present knowledge
of dwindling time
serves as the partition
that both pushes
and pulls
everything apart
and
together again.

# 618. Untitled - 2002.01.17

Like the silent night
gradually emptying the sky
of bright lights
and the noise
of daytime -
the slow dance of two lives
begins.

In time, you stole my words,
replacing them with joy -
overflowing from the heart
until they found haven
on new pages.

In silence, I revel
at the new sensations -
unable to give voice
to all that was felt --
knowing only
that this was pure
and utter
happiness.

# 619. Untitled - 2002.01.17

T'is with negligent grace
that I watch the grown up kitten
purr with increased intensity -
an eloquent song
of happiness and satisfaction.

The merest of murmurs
casts away the grumpy dealings
of the day,
continuing until
all the worries are cast aside.

As the kitten
frolics with great abandon,
I am persuaded
to relinquish the weary day
and play into welcome night.

# 620. Untitled - 2002.01.17

It was the sweet taste of
sensation
that changed everything,
even as everyone else
receded into the background.

The feel of smooth silk
against warm hands
caused a cascade of
scintillating reverberations
across the nerves.

All I could remember
are the remnants of a smile -
it sends the spirits
into a heavenly spiral.

# 621. 2002.01.18

The heavenly scent
of fresh baked bread
does battle against
the visual pleasure
of fulfillment.

The ringed loaf
is a combination of
desire and satiation
even before
a single bite is taken.

Liberally covered by
a dusting of powdered sweetness,
the right is weighed down
by the many slivers
of crisp almonds.

As the fragrance wafts
beyond the immediate,
a row of elfin faces
gathers in anticipation
of a tasty treat.

**622.** 2002.01.18

Even in the crowded spaces,
I feel alone;
even as the voices are raised in laughter,
I don't feel their joy.

There is an emptiness
that echoes within -
a sense of want
that hides the sadness felt.

A shroud of detachment
muffles the white noise
surrounding me.

Time doesn't pass fast enough
these days...

Slow down, speed up -
time gets away from me;
I count the moments
until we meet again.

**623.** 2002.01.18

Like the bloom
of a fresh cut rose,
everything gains
a new perspective
and dreams are
no longer impossible.

Time becomes both
the soil that nourishes life;
and the air that
dries the silken petals.

**624.** 2002.01.18

A handful of white candies
spill across the glass -
scattering into a million
patterns.

A deft touch
causes them to roll
back and forth -
wavering in so many directions.

Every candy melts away,
until the almond center
is revealed.

## 625. 2002.01.19

T'is bittersweet knowledge
to see the arrival of a priceless
gift
matched by the loss of equal
measure.

Every move made,
ripples outwards
until all the land is changed.

Every word said
or unsaid
changes meaning
by its presence
or the lack thereof.

So many things left unsaid
until its too late -
so many choices left unmade
until there are none remaining.

## 626. 2002.01.19

The pure silence lulls -
rocking gently against
the beckoning sleep.

As breathing slows
and the night deepens -
other sounds replace
the bustle of the daylight living.

It's with a slow, gradual
detachment of the mind
from the worries of the day
that dreams become
the norm once more.

Floating from one dream cloud
to the next,
everything gains an ethereal
shadow -
muting all the coloured tones
of the mind.

## 627. 2002.01.19

Two lifetimes pass in the blink
of an eye,
one moment of joy matched by
one moment of sorrow.

Everything is separated by
a before and after -
a world once black and grey
replaced by the many hues
of the rainbow -
both happiness and sadness
cast in blues and reds.

Every sunset remembered
was a wonderful mix
of lush violets and orange.

Every day passed was bright lit
with golden sunshine
and pale blue skies.

Even as the night sky grew dark,
the white snowflakes
reflected
the myriad of colours.

## 628. 2002.01.20

It's a sliding scale
of like and love -
where does one end,
and the other start?

In a pattern of black and white,
why so many shades of grey?

## 629. 2002.01.20

What starts as a
leisurely trip
across the hilly state
becomes a slow meandering
through every nook and cranny.

Stopping time and time again
to watch the pale peach and pink hues
dust hillocks and distant shadows.

In a moment of impulse,
a deft touch of the fingers
shifts all gears upwards -
bringing the subtle hum
to a sub-vocal roar of pleasure.

Moments pass quickly
even as the surfaces grow slick
and the sense of anticipation increases -
where the danger of crashing
vies with the thrill of the ride.

## 629. 2002.01.20

As the waves of water
gently lap against the shore,
the sun sets in a brilliant burst of colour -
a golden ball of flame
against the deep magenta sky.

The crunch of the sand and
pebbles is loud
against the silence of the day.
Every step on the shifting beach
is a indelible imprint for the moment.

The high tide
rushes back in
and washes away
the light prints made.

A sigh filled with longing
is heard hanging sharply
on the memories of a time past.

## 630. 2002.01.22

In the lingering silence,
large watery bunny eyes
silently tug
at the strings of sympathy...

Continuing the emphatic stare
until you can't help
but look away,
a soft sigh
is breathed aloud,
as all resistance
falls to pieces.

## 631. 2002.01.23

In an endless moment
where all breathing stops
and silence grows thick -
eyes are smitten
by the sight
of pure,
liquid
sweetness
gradually
oozing
from the hard chocolate shell.

As the wee truffle
spills out
onto waiting nibbles,
a hum begins
and becomes
a soft moan
of satisfaction.

## 632. 2002.01.24

With a bluntness found
refreshing,
more than cryptic allusions
are laid to the wayside,
and direct questions asked once
more.

In another round
of both subtle
and non - probing,
searching, querying,
there is no pain felt
as the answers lead
to another end.

## 633. 2002.01.26

As the evening fog
rolls in from the Bay,
the streetlamps cast
hazy trails
on wet roads.

Through the mist arises
a lone bus stop,
barren, but for
the lone person
waiting
for the sun to set.

The pitter-patter of the raindrops
was muffled in the dark,
echoing eerily against
hollow stones.

## 634. 2002.01.26

The rocking motion
both lulls
and hearkens us
to the rhythm of the train -
even when it's crowded,
both memories and time
have created
a sphere of silence -
where the train
takes us into the past -
living sweet memories
once more.

Every moment becomes
forgotten
as the rumble of every wheel
crosses the metal track -
rhythmically hypnotizing
until we reached
the final destination.

## 635. 2002.01.28

It is with equal intensity
that I feel every gain
and every loss,
turning over every word
and reaction
for meanings inherent
and implicit.

It is with the knowledge
of the power of words
that keeps me silent -
saying few
but leaving even more
unsaid.

It is the truth
that sets me free -
to speak what was left unsaid;
to write what was left
unread.

## 636. 2002.01.29

The scent of sweet apples
wafts in gentle gusts
from the warm kitchen
until a hunger
rises from within.

Bedazzled by the sheer beauty
and simplicity
of the crisp crumble topping,
every bite becomes
a mélange of tastes -
both sweet and tangy.

The hums of pleasure
ring in the ears
of even those
in the depths of sleeping -
roused, just to feed
this insatiable hunger.

## 637. 2002.01.30

As the night falls,
the perception changes
from light to dark,
from now to then,
from here to there.

Every word that sounded harsh
in daylight
gains a new interpretation in
moonlight -
words imbued with meaning
unheard.

If it's any consolation,
every smile is worth
all the changes in place.

## 638. 2002.01.31

The snow falls heavily
from the sky
as the wee figures
saunter across the road.

A small smile creeps across
closed eyes
at the prospect of returning
from the howling cold
to the warm of a burning fire.

The crystalline silence
of the snowflakes falling
is broken by the sound
of a slow sip of warm cocoa.

## 639. 2002.02.02

- Addicted to Speed (They went
past the limits again and again!)

It's a single point in the
landscape
that catches our eyes -
slowly meandering across
slick surfaces.

Exquisite silence is felt inside
even as the warm winds
blow across blue skies -
casting pale pink
and dusty rose
as fleshy tones.

The scent of intangible wonder
mixes in with the danger of the
moment
as hidden hands find their way
into the hot pockets of flesh
covered by cool leather.

Every touch
serving to notch up the moment
with infinitesimal desire.

As the touch becomes slower,
the desire to speed ahead climbs
higher,
until a blinding whiteness
obviates all else,
and all that is important
is the cool touch
of the real rider
of this sleek machine.

## 640. 2002.02.04

Like pure nougat melting
onto waiting buds -
the taste of peanut butter
crawls slowly
from biscuit
to tongue
in the slow sensation
of ecstasy.

Every bite and every nibble
never fully fades from memory
before we are bombarded
with slick sweetness
once more.

Licking the fingers in
satisfaction,
it tickles the fancy
to imagine devouring the next
cookie.

## 641. 2002.02.08

In the bright city lights
where shadow lives shelter,
a slow dance of two hearts begins
-
meeting once in the past,
rejoining in the present,
seeking to create a future.

Like a giant chess game of skill
and wits
with matching point and
counterpoint,
each move is met
by a million possibilities -
each one endless in dreams.

Even as they are speeding
towards
an unknown destiny,
the sound of laughter
floating far behind,
every day slows down -
wanting to savour every moment
possible.

Like a moth drawn to the bright
lit flame,
the conflagration of passion
burns,
bringing them to their knees in a
fury -
only to be left yearning for more.

## 642. 2002.02.09

On every question asked,
an answer is given -
never quite expected,
never quite complete.

Crossing the Rubicon
in saying more
by saying less -
every word becomes another
reason
to pontificate on the why and
wherefores.

Every moment passing
becomes a step-stone
in the renewal
of the thirst for knowledge.

## 643. 2002.02.09

In the nearing of spring,
the snow melts
to reveal patches of verdant grass
beyond the boundary of just
white.

The days grow longer
in the happy reunion
of light and warmth.217

## 644. 2002.02.10

- Biker Babes

It is the merest of touches
ventured across supple silk
that causes everything to
contract -
not another breath ventured -
every nerve awaiting
the very next stroke.

It's the scintillating hum of
approval
that causes every nuance to
stabilize -
attentive to the passing
moments.

The spinning tires churn against
the yielding asphalt
even as the grip is firm
against the elastic leather.

The roar of the engine rises
and then peaks
as the shadowed riders
disappear in the sunrise.

## 645. 2002.02.14

By the merest of seconds,
the fear that hides
around the next corner
of ribboned ice
slides away
like the fast
of luge sliders
hurtling
down the slick track.

Faster and faster,
everyone moves
to deliver
on that golden moment
where lose
was conquered
by hope.

Separated by the distance
of a pinkie
between first
and oblivion,
spirits soar
on that last word: go!

## 646. 2002.02.19

The cool air parts effortlessly
as the slick sounds
fall upon waiting ears.

In seemingly aimless
twists and turns,
catch the glow
of a million lights
reflecting in the glimmer
of a smile
that peaks out from
behind closed eyes.

Cutting through the smooth
glaze
of frozen moments,
the mind swoons
as the last second
reveals an icy kiss
from a force of nature.

## 647. 2002.02.20

The purity of vision
for one who is blind,
is deafening
like thunder across the night
skies.

In a gradual movement
away from the centre
of all that has happened,
the light becomes less in
meaning.

Eventually, there is no loss,
but the glimmer of remembrance
against the memories of the days
gone by.

## 648. 2002.03.13

Bright sunlight deflects
off of pale marble,
even as endless motion
carves away
to create simple lines
against liquid forms.

Peeling away
to reveal classical lines
until the time comes
to begin the task
of giving form to flesh,
replacing layers
with smooth silk
then leather.

## 649. 2002.03.20

From a stream of consciousness
come pearls of words
flowing unrelentingly
from an endless spring
of inspiration
until the time came
that the rivers ran dry,
and the stream
became a trickle
'til it was no more.

A silent search begins
for both reason
and the cause
of words unbidden,
leaping from thought
to page.

Until pearls ground to dust
merging once more
with the earth.

Only time continued on,
wearing away at endless forces,
revealing one day,
small sparkles found
in diamond phrases
fewer in number
than before.

## 650. 2002.03.29

Can't break what's not there,
can't lose what was never won,
can't find what was never
hidden.

Silence begins and ends in the
moment,
stolen from a time or twenty,
it becomes the cloak,
then the mantle
to rest upon.

Shrouded and hidden,
moving from shadow to shadow,
blending in perfect harmony,
to the unheard echoes.

## 651. 2002.03.29

Against a million raindrops
the city lights reflect,
a shimmer of brightness
against the dark night sky.

The distant sound of cars
splashing through the rain
breaks the silence
that fell across the moment.

## 652. 2002.03.30

The strange glitter of raindrops
are the reflections
of a dragon's tears,
falling in silent majesty
from hidden golden eyes.

A pearly sheen
cast in pale moonlight,
dragon-tears fade away
in the harsh sun
of the morning.

The luminescent shine serves
as the only remembrance
of the hint of a dragon's smile -
wryly bittersweet
in this molten moment.

## 653. 2002.03.31

Making pictures with just words,
drawing lines by pushing
shadows into light,
finding silence within pure
chaos,
finding light in the middle of
darkness.

Shading black against pure
white,
hearing silence in a cacophony
of voices,
seeing nothing in the multitude
of colours,
leaving emptiness as the
unwanted gift.

## 654. 2002.04.01

When words are not enough,
and speech is too fragile,
grasping for meaning
from the thought
of empty promises
makes everything run together
into a morass of confusion
and utter silence.

Open mouthed
but voiceless,
open to all the things
visceral to our living,
thinking of what might have
been,
looking at what could be.

This contradiction
in living and hoping
leaves too many questions
unanswered,
words meant for the ears
of another
remain unspoken.

## 655. 2002.04.05

Time is of an essence
seldom gained but always lost.

Every moment passing
into oblivion,
lost before it's even found.

A silent march
into the dark unknowing,
pacing oneself
for an endless time.

## 656. 2002.04.05

In absolute silence,
the shattering clarify
of faith in the intangible
becomes the overwhelming
reality,
even as it gives way
to some facet of truth
versus fiction.

Every moment
becomes a slow motion
picture of a thousand words
even as no words are spoken.

Let no false truths
and half hopes
become the basis
of an illusion
that has no end.

## 657. 2002.04.06

In the harsh light
of the morning sun,
a certain clarity
is cast upon
thoughts voiced
in the hazy shadows
of midnight.

Reality has not changed
but more pieces are brought to
light.

Emptiness is not filled
by light,
passing through
and leaving all
in the same moment.

## 658. 2002.04.10

It's never truly darkness
but that of a shadow cast
by an event that crosses
the threshold
of the heart.

Pictures that once stood
in vivid contrast against
a life of grey,
fade once more
into the shades of black and
white.

Every sound heard in the silence
is an eerie reminder
of things once said -
every nuance clear as the
dawning
of the next day.

Even as the internal warmth
seeps away,
the sunlight outside
is a brilliant remembrance
of the happiness
once shared.

## 659. 2002.04.10

The cost one pays
for faith and security
is beyond the measure
of our lives.

The cost one bears
for hope and eternity
is beyond the words
of our world.

## 660. 2002.04.10

The late afternoon shadows
give way
to the evening glow
as the last rays of light
fade within the gradual
tinges of pink
and deep purple.

The shifting border
between day and night
reveals the receding veil
of reality and myth.

## 661. 2002.04.11

What begins as a mild touch
against the unsuspecting,
is a subtle reminder
of the many nuances
that rule our lives.

Every bit carves away
at pale stone
until it becomes
an undulating ocean
of blood red
and bright crimson.

Every welt raised
rubs against smooth silk,
resting lightly against
scarred flesh.

The surface twitches
in response to the passing
breeze,
aching for some relief
to this nascent mixture
of pleasurable pain.

## 662. 2002.04.12

Every word falls
like an unexploded grenade
across a broken field
where the soil is rent
beyond belief.

March across the countryside
searching for hidden losses,
gingerly avoid the known,
only to be destroyed
at the next crossing point.

## 663. 2002.04.13

What began as a meeting
in a world of 1s and 0s
viable only through words
and writing
met in the middle
in a flurry of words
that poured unrelenting
from a fount once hidden.

Until all the words
disappeared
in an ephemeral moment,
where all the feelings
became unimportant once more.

## 664. 2002.04.16

Every word told a story,
ever phrase - a turn in time,
every thought became
a study in prose,
even as
words became not enough
to capture that moment -
fleeting in nature,
hidden in time.

## 665. 2002.04.30

Darkness is but shadows made,
gathered from too many corners.
Rolling like tumbleweed
across the empty expanse.

Emptiness becomes a reflection,
of all that is not within;
barred from the silence
that lasts from dawn
to dusk.

## 666. 2002.05.05

The spring breeze
pushes the last vestiges
of sleep
from the dreams
of the somnolent.

The grey shadows
that begin the morning
give way
to hazy sunshine
peeking from behind
fluffy clouds.

## 667. 2002.05.11

Taking solace
in the blanket of silence
that covers all things
at all times.

Seeking moments
where not speaking is treasured,
all thoughts are tethered,
and nothing is as it seems.

In alternating shadows
of lightness,
and dark,
this silence truly speaks
to life
both quiet,
and stark.

## 668. 2002.05.11

Three words -
all one would want to hear,
yet not hear at the same time.

To three simple words -
I had just three for that moment
-
and not the ones you'd want to
hear,
nor the ones I'd wish to say -
"I do not."

In this vacuum of words,
there is too much
left unexplained,
yet there are no words
to justify
the truth of what was.

## 669. 2002.05.20

It's a stately dance
with an edge of danger,
moving back and forth
across the abyss.

Two-stepping across the gaps
that exist before and hereafter -
until the great game of life
mimics this dance.

Giving and taking,
spinning towards
and away
at the same time.

Following a hidden beat
that syncopates
at random moments
until the cacophony of noise
resounds in life.

## 670. 2002.05.20

It's a silken surface
that moves from
cool softness
to heated tension.

Shifting from
languid lethargy
that colours
the early morning hours
to the turgid tension
that stretches the moment
into an endless search
for senseless satiation.

## 671. 2002.05.23

Along the hidden paths
that dot the lush green hills,
an echoing laughter is heard.

Resounding from the valley
up into the hillsides
are the silvery chimes of joy.

The spring mornings
see wet dew cascading
across the surface
of small pools of water,
until it becomes a torrent
of sheer liquidity
crashing through
the silence of creeks
and valleys.

The bright sunlight
reflects easily across
the running waters,
until it mirrors
the slight smile
running across your lips.

## 672. 2002.05.23

Hazy dusk settles into gentle
twilight
as the shadows stretch long and
low.

A musical trill runs down the
mountain
hiding behind the moon-cast
shades.

As daylight gives way to
moonshine,
sounds become more acute -
until all we can hear
are the subtle voices
of the hidden folk here.

## 673. 2002.06.01

Falling into a field
of spring daffodils -
surrounded
by a million hues
of yellow sunshine.

The petal softness
becomes the first layer of touch
against the sun-kissed nipples.

A slash of saffron
reveals a slight smile,
brilliant against
the early morning shadows.

Every daffodil dolefully sways
against the breeze
that ruffles their edges,
and hums the morning song.

## 674. 2002.06.01

Like an endless stream
of droplets
against a rocky shelf,
time wears away
at the surface layers
until a groove runs
deep and wide.

Gradually, the distance widens
until that's all there is
remaining -
a gap that once was.

## 675. 2002.06.02

It is a subtle measure of vengeance
that is slowly being wrought,
jibes and jabs,
snips and snaps.

Gradually, there is no humour
to laugh it all away.
A sign of "death by a thousand cuts"
where words are both -
not enough to heal,
yet,
more than enough to wound.

Once more into the breach,
where silence is the armour,
and knowledge the only sword.

Another dance
of parry, parry, riposte
has begun.

## 676. 2002.06.04

First six, then nine.
First yours, then mine.

Here now, there later,
live first, dream later.

The beginning meets the end,
then flips over to begin again.

What's here but gone again,
what's gone but fear of them.

First nine, then six,
first sight, no tricks.

Later "then" is now here,
laughter begins and ends with tears.

First now, last then;
six, nine, but no tens.

## 677. 2002.06.05

Wielding words like the flaming blade,
every clash is a resounding silence,
cutting remarks are no defense
against the implied and unspoken.

Subterfuge becomes the mode of battle -
undermining whatever might have been.

Presumptions broken;
shattered in a sudden storm,
wreck and ruin
left in its wake.

## 678. 2002.06.07

There is the interminable silence
that overpowers every word
spoken.

There is the semblance of naked
awkwardness
that dominates every moment
passing.

Like the grains of sand,
falling carelessly towards
the hourglass bottom -
every second passes
unmarked in time.

An evening chill
envelopes the night sky,
devoid of all warmth
and light.

## 679. 2002.06.08

The hot summer heat
beats down on black pavement
until the steam rises slowly
into the shimmering haze.

Slowly,
falling forward
as the white frothing cream,
cool to the touch
and sweet to the taste.

Tracing patterns
of white stickiness
against a writhing landscape
until no crevice
is left unfilled
in a living work
of art.

## 680. 2002.06.09

Hot black vulcanized rubber
hugs a slick wet surface,
grappling with unrelenting
strength
as the speed increases
until all you're living for,
is the moment,
where everything moves
at the speed of sound
yet slows down
to infinite split seconds.

The exhilaration becomes
the reason for speed -
moving beyond the boundaries
into the infinite horizon of light.

Riding that thin edge
of control,
a hairs width away
from falling
into
an endless canyon of
airlessness,
and knowing that
falling
is just what you want.

Slipping and sliding
along black rubber,
grasping and gripping
for that elusive
control.
The moment this race
to the finish ends,
the need driving everything
roars again,
the end and the beginning
meet once more.

## 681. 2002.06.09

Like a vivid colour
against dull grey,
the sunlight
becomes a single beam
into all the shadows.

Like a raindrop,
the moments fall
and then scatter
into a million shards
of possibilities
and "what might have beens."

Like the snowflakes,
the thought dissipates
under the heat
of the morning sun.

## 682. 2002.06.11

The taste of water
is ambrosia
to the desert travelers,
poison to the flooded,
and a paradise
of sweetness for those
that only hear of it.

The taste of water
becomes the elusive treasure
that reminds us
of the purity
of the moment
once sullied
cannot be returned.

## 683. 2002.06.13

In a circle of truth,
very little is kept hidden
from the others
in our life.

Strengthened by the knowledge
that the edge
separating
the without,
from within
can become an infinite line
circling our lives
in a continuous song.

Bound by a thread of energy
that is nourished by love
and rooted in friendship,
the circle centers
the lives within.

## 684. 2002.06.14

In the midst of the pouring rain,
the world is reflected in the shine
of a million raindrops --
cooling the lives
caught standing
in the night storm.

As the droplets slide
across an unmoving face,
a million expressions cross
hurriedly
in the pale moonlight.

Just as quickly as the storm
moves in,
it disappears,
only the waiting remains
as the receding moonlight
seeks shelter
away from prying eyes.

## 685. 2002.06.14

Peeling away the layers
of our soul,
gradually forcing the reality
upon our senses -
the realization that life
is beyond the present;
stretching into the metaphysics
of things that we cannot
understand.

Like a million shades of colour,
that created a vivid landscape;
every moment reveals another
aspect
of our lives lived -
one more facet of the soul.

Like the diamond held
infinitely precious;
every turn in the sun
casts both shadow and light
upon the secret corners
of our life.

## 686. 2002.06.15

Cherry lips
become the point
of focus
for all the sunlight
peeking through
the dappled shade.

Pressing a string of kisses
against barren skin,
the rouge cerise smudges
slowly
until it traces
the hallows of the flesh.

## 687. Untitled - 2002.06.17

In a slow motion picture
of black and white
I watched the world
gradually turn
in time
to the silent beats
of music only heard
by those closest
to the group of dancers.

In a universal song
for peace,
a measure was sought
and found
in the minutes
that passed by
so gradually.

The voice of a song
sung so long ago,
yet never losing
a moments meaning
even twenty years
after he first sang.

In clear unison
the movements
slowed to an end.

## 688. Untitled - 2002.06.18

Every drop of white
slowly meanders
across crevices of golden tan,
glisteningly sweet
in the hot sun above.

The gradual melting
from frozen coolness
into a liquid bounty
is contrasted
to the frail crisp of a flesh
soaked in sugared sweetness
until it begins to melt
in the hand
of the beholder.

Sharp nips,
and soft licks
move the mound of white
deeper into gold hallows
until is disappears unto
a point.

As the summer sun
beats down on the heavy
afternoon,
a desperate race between
taste and time
ensues,
ensuring that the ice cream
is gone ~
remembered only
by the tasting of smooth
fingers.

## 689. Untitled - 2002.06.19

Sleep is a long time coming
in the quietest hours of the
night,
where the silence that surrounds
you
makes every breath sound that
much louder.

Every twist, and every turn
brings no relief in sight,
magnifying the very fact
that you're awaiting the return to
light.

In the darkness
broken only by the waning
streetlights,
all the white noise
moves to the foreground,
playing counterpart
to the jumble of thoughts
that run through our mind.

Even when eyes are closed,
the mind runs wild,
snippets of the past crashing
through the emptiness
strived for.

Slow breaths, deep sighs,
and absolute silence
gradually serve
to ease the mind;
only to awaken again
to the knowledge
that dawn has come
once again.

## 690. Untitled - 2002.06.21

Like a pane of glass
falling
from high above the floor,
everything shatters
into a million pieces
sparkling in the sunlight.

Meeting a thousand faces
each wanting something
different,
until the soul splinters
and reforms into
someone new.

Every moment
is new ~
every expectation is different;
every person met
becomes one more tug
in a different direction.

## 691. Untitled - 2002.06.22

In a moment of silence,
everything changed -
how telling
in the knowledge
that pure truth
was in silence.

How the truth
became reality
with words left unspoken,
although hearts
could not be unbroken.

What was the past
but a collection of moments -
each more ethereal than the next
-
neither continuous nor collected
were they;
providing an illusory foundation
for the ever-changing present.

## 692. Untitled - 2002.06.22

In the hot haze
that marks the early days of
summer,
we are drenched with sweat
that slides downwards
in a wet path
leaving watching eyes captivated.

In the sudden storms
that break the heat,
the rain comes down
in a matter of minutes,
and everything is soaked to the
skin -
a welcome change
from the sheen of dust
that coated the early day.

As the downpour continues,
the rain softens to become
a soothing balm
to the soul.

The clash of thunder and
lightning
becomes the drumbeat
for a sudden frenzy
of energetic dancing -
like a whirling dervish
chasing the hidden dreams.

In this euphoric pleasure -
the sky is lit up
by jags of white lightning -
glistening off your laughing eyes.

As the dance ends, and your shy
smile becomes,
I realize
that the most gorgeous thing
here,
were these moments of freedom
in the summer rain.

## 693. Untitled - 2002.06.22

It is a hidden moment,
unseen by many
that marks the crossing
of the look of bliss -
a smile of happiness
that soothes the soul,
lighting the eyes from within.

In a cloud of euphoria,
all that is heard
in the afternoon silence
is the subtle pursing
of sweet lips -
glisteningly wet
as a flurry of soft kisses
dot the pale landscape
lazing in the summer sun.

Rising from a hallowed grotto,
drenched with salty sweat,
fierce eyes
rake back and forth
across the path less travelled
to reveal a satisfied smile
changing the meaning
of gorgeous
once more.

## 694. Untitled - 2002.06.23

It is one breath
that separates
one moment from the next;
the difference in hearing
that hitched sound of
expectation
or the pained gasp of ending.

It's the one last breath
that marks both a beginning
and the end;
where the past and present meet.

Every heartbeat passing
begins a secondary cycle
of listening for the sounds
of a sharp intake of air -
in both pleasure and pain -
in a time of suspended
living.

## 695. Untitled - 2002.06.24

The air is thick with anticipation
as a breath hitches
in a moment of shared solitude;
held until it becomes
a slow hiss of pleasure.

In the distance,
a low rumble of thunder
rolling in from the ocean centre;
as it nears,
the electricity of the moment
seems to be transferred
directly to fingertips
found hovering,
just above.

A flash of lightning
arches from the sky,
eerily reflected
in the piercing need
that leaves everything jagged.

As the sudden storm recedes,
a lingering cascade of tears
is wiped away,
as the simple smile seen
seems to be a path
drawn to forever.

## 696. Mixed Metaphors - 2002.06.24

Everything began as a lark -
with no time like the present
to play the only game in town.

In a twist of fate,
the trials and tribulations
of every armchair quarterback
couldn't
 even get to first base
in the dog days of summer
never mind make its way
onto the infamous hidden
agenda.

Taking the plunge
instead of throwing in the towel,
the phrase of "look before you leap"
took on a different intent and
purpose.

So it was,
that we once were
young and foolish,
eschewing the wisdom of the ages
for the shroud
of existentialist angst,
filled with Freudian slips
even as we
laid claim to this being
just fun and games.236

## 697. Untitled - 2002.06.26

The ink spills
onto white linen -
soaking into the fabric,
held tightly forever.

The words struggle
across the page,
jostling for position
and prominence.

The emptiness is glaring,
splayed apart
for all to see,
and none to notice.

## 698. Untitled - 2002.06.28

There is no true death
in the words given away.
Remembered and savoured
like the finest of wines
on the tip of my tongue,
they remain engraved
with the meanings
ever-changing and transformed.

Like the inevitable
ebbing of the tide,
the words and vowels
rise and fall
with the passing of time,
crashing vividly
against the sea
of imagination.

## 699. Untitled - 2002.06.28

When the words fall downwards
into an unending spiral,
where all the thoughts
are focused
on the same
point in time,
then everything rushes
to the forefront.

Every word is like a window,
peering into a hidden world,
seeing the myriad of images
evoked by a single moment.

The changes around every
corner
are bound by the reality
within.

Until the nuances read by
another
changes life
once again.

## 700. Untitled - 2002.06.28

Peeking behind the veil,
and seeing through the shadows;
every moment
becomes meaningful
for that hidden sign.

Every slick slide,
every careless nibble,
was it just ice cream,
or something more?

Every opening becomes a cavern,
every mound becomes a mountain,
every ride becomes an adventure.

## 701. Untitled - 2002.06.28

Where every moment
of anticipation
carries an underlying layer of
anxiety,
any performance becomes
magnified
by the knowledge
that countless eyes
are watching
and reading
the end results.

The salty remnants of tears -
whether from joy
or exhaustion,
slide slowly
downwards,
kissed away
by a moment's hesitation,
and carried off
in a slight flick of the tongue.

As fingertips hover
against pearl white,
expectations are on the verge
of exploding outwards,
pouring into a rapid fire
cascade of touches,
until all that is left,
are the black and white images
imbedded on simple white,
leaving the receiver breathless,
and the giver exhilarated.

## 701. Untitled - 2002.06.29

Gathered
along the lower extents of
yielding streets is a buzzing
sound.

Perfect rows of laughing
riders that indulge in the
innocence of the last minutes of
desperate preparation -- wiping
down glistening
engines proudly.

Parallel travelers
arrive at the destination, filled
with
remonstrations of
avid and fiercely visible joy,
donning (or shedding) their
cloak of leather against
everything, and nothing at all.

## 496. Untitled - June 30, 2002

It's the thin layer of darkness
barely covering the frozen middle,
that melts under the summer heat.

Every cut
breaking the smooth surface
sinking slowly into a thick haze
of sweetness
until you hit rock bottom;
and the path is reversed
to exposed the underlying coldness
to the world.

The chill is a pleasant surprise
against the sweet layers in between,
lingering in the memory,
until everything else melts away.

## 702. Untitled - 2002.06.30

It is a fine line
between pleasure and pain,
trod carefully
against the edge of reason.

Every pinch
leaves an indelible mark
against soft skin,
rawly red
against pale flesh.

The small twinges of pain
build until
it is indecipherable
from the pleasure
of the small touches
against the skin.

## 703. Untitled - 2002.06.30

Every flex of the muscles
causes the entire spine
to undulate in pleasure.

Watching the majestic dragon
climb up the flesh
towards the range
of small hills
and valleys
until it is seated
just under
and against the shoulders;
carefully hidden
away
from the sight
of prying eyes.

## 704. Untitled - 2002.06.30

The height of the summer sun
beats unrelentingly
on the glaring pates
unshorn in the sweltering heat.

The lure of the cool waters
beckons endlessly
until the oasis
shimmers in the heavy heat.

## 705. 2002.07.02

As the sun sets
in a fiery haze of red,
the heat is unforgiving
in its harshness.

The need
to simply surrender
against the blazing warmth
is dulled
by the slick feel
of icy coldness
against the surface.

Slowly,
everything melts
under the heat,
gradually forming a pool
of sweet liquid -
that is yielding
to the touch.

Every dab,
every flickered look
garners another -
until it becomes
an unceasing
need for contact
against heated flesh.

## 706. Untitled - 2002.07.06

Like the gradual fading
of the evening sky
into the dark of night,
everything sinks deeper
into perspective.

The dusk haze
gives way to darkness -
until there is nothing left
but ink blackness
swallowing everything
within.

## 707. Untitled - 2002.07.06

Absinthe makes the mind forget
all the things
that make life worth living.

Finding wisdom
at the bottom of a glass,
finding oblivion
in every sip swallowed.

Clarity sought
in every drop;
but reality fades
replaced by emptiness found.

## 708. Untitled - 2002.07.06

The solid embrace
of clear cut crystal
filled with liquid gold
becomes solace
against all that is
beyond the now
and the here.

Slow sips,
quick gulps,
all serve to make things
come away with greater speed
than before.

Every moment,
becomes a march towards
both oblivion
and forgetfulness.

Verbal brilliance
becomes a thing of past
as words become slurred
and garbled
in the confusion that reigns.

The half glass
is but a sign
beckoning
to be filled again.

Heads clear,
hearts full,
are but what is left
of lives lived.

## 709. Untitled - 2002.07.07

It's an endless marathon
being run,
twenty-six miles
after twenty-six miles.

The terrain is rough,
and never of our choosing,
no byways and highways
to distract from the end.

The long distance runner
becomes but a speck
in the horizon
that never fades.

Every footstep
becomes a moment
away from the start,
towards the unknown;
every heartbeat
becomes a marker
against the winding time.

Running like hell,
but going no where,
that is the marathon
in circles.

## 710. Untitled - 2002.07.07

The choice of no choosing;
where every race run
becomes one without a start
nor an end.

Options masquerade
as reality;
and illusion
becomes the truth.

The white flag flails
even as spirits fail;
for why run,
when there is no solution
in sight.

## 711. Untitled - 2002.07.08

The race is never won,
for life is never done.
The soul is weary,
as the future is bleary.

There is no choice left to make
but to run ahead, and claim our
stake,
until everything becomes a blur.

Another case of perpetual
motion
without any progress;
movement for the sake thereof.

## 712. Untitled - 2002.07.08

The pendulum begins
to swing backwards,
into the past,
away from the future.

Forwards,
sideways,
backwards again,
minute movements
that leave us standing still.

There is no progress to be
marked;
there is no need to reach for the
impossible;
for the search is laid to rest.

Conceding the race
before it's run;
retreating from life
before it's done.

## 713. Untitled - 2002.07.08

Why live a life of clichés
when there are roads less
traveled?

Why live for tomorrow
when today is an age of torment?

Why search for glories from afar,
when butterflies are miracles in
flight?

Ultimately,
the road chosen
may not have risen to meet us
at all.


## 714. Untitled - 2002.07.08

It's a constant search in life,
for the beauty that claims to lie
within;
for so many have learnt
to do without.

It's a constant struggle to balance
the good with the bad,
the here and the now
with the past and the future.

It's a moment in time stolen
when I watch
the butterflies dance.


## 715. Untitled - 2002.07.10

The bright sunlight of July
filters through the windows,
broken only by the swaying
of the summer breeze
amongst the trees.

The low hum that fills the
background
is loud against the silence
that is the outside world;
intersected by
the dull roar of cars
in the distance.

The searing heat
that filled the week
has given way
to a cooler clime
that lets us enjoy the sun
without melting away.

The wind picks up
and the outdoors beckon
for an afternoon
of dozing in the sun,
until the evening shadows
cast their way
across the heated surface.

# 716. Untitled - 2002.07.10

A cool tall glass
of clarity rests
against the grained wood bar.

Every sip becomes a relief;
soothing the hunger
that gnaws within.

In the smoky darkness,
awareness fades away
until night blends into day,
and summer/winter seasons
do not differ.

Even as a sip is taken,
the waves outside
crash against the boardwalk,
drowning out
the sycophant cries
of seagulls
and other ocean flocks.

The rush of excitement
that begins the turning of the tide
loses strength
and ebbs away
under the brilliant moonlight.

# 717. Untitled - 2002.07.11

Like the Ancient Mariner
perched upon the cliffs,
waiting becomes life,
watching becomes living,
and sometimes
reality becomes like a dream.

Even as the ocean waves
pound away against
the sandy beaches,
the gradual erosion
of land
against water
is happening
against the tide.

Eventually
the island disappears
from the sea,
its particulates carried away
into the unknown
and deposited
against a distant shore.

Falling inwards
into the watery depths
where clarity
and darkness
are one and the same;
where inky blue waters
become the sun-filled surface.

The oceans become
the one constant;
filling, emptying
into itself;
running through a cycle
of destruction
then rejuvenation,
continuing until
it is emptied
one day.

## 718. Untitled - 2002.07.11

The absolute resilience
of the spirit
is the one true miracle
in life;
beyond all others,
is the knowledge
that there is no depth
that cannot
be surmounted.

The footprints
upon the beach sands
are washed away
by the receding tide;
withdrawing
the cloud of weariness
from around us
until all that is left
is a soul
refreshed
and ready
to do battle once more
against the waves
that would wash
us away.

## 719. Untitled - 2002.07.11

The connection
that holds the soul
within this world
is neither love
nor money;
but that of the memory;
once golden in happiness;
then silvered in age;
until all that remains
are faded shadows
of what once was.

The depth of the times past
are the anchors
that hold a life lived
in reverence and solemnity.

Memories created
in both life and fiction;
living onwards in words spoken,
pictures taken,
and occasions that were
the high/low points of life.

The passing is hastened
in this time,
by the gradual disappearance
of the milestones
that marked a life;
no pictures remain,
nor many words remain,
until the whisper of a name
is all that is left
to connect
between
this world
and the next.

## 720. Untitled - 2002.07.12

If a picture is worth a thousand
words,
then let there be no images
but those carved
on white stone
with black ink.

Like a pinhole view,
let time fade
the memories
until only the words remain.

Let the words speak for
themselves,
for that moment captured in
time,
and carefully released
to the world.

## 721. Untitled - 2002.07.15

Every light becomes a dream
freed from the confines
of the mind.

A wild dance in the darkest of
hours,
where the stars are hazy
in the moonlit sky,
becomes a reflection
of the effervescent moment -
of a million creatures
in tune with life around them,
and dancing because they can.

The cloud of fireflies
surrounds everything,
sharing illumination
with the night.

This captured light
becomes a hopeful dream
of a child sleeping away,
remembering the moment
where joy and laughter
came alive once more.

## 722. Untitled - 2002.07.15

It's the life beat of nature
that beckons us to dance;
to find the joy
that would give us
more laughter.

The sweetest of babes
find pleasure in life,
for all the simplicity
that is seen.

It's only as we grow,
"older" and "wiser"
that we gradually lose
sight of what's importance,
and focus too often
on what should be
and isn't.

Only on the evenings
where the night skies are clear
can we lie back
and dream of what is,
counting the stars
and playing amongst
the june bugs
until we remember back
to life as it once was.

## 723. Untitled - 2002.07.15

As the drumbeats sound,
and the lights flash away,
the sudden beats of bass
draw from within
this urge
to match moments
with a hidden song
and a forgotten song.

Ancient steps
around a sun stone
remind us
of the times
where wisdom came with age,
and fools
weren't just those young at heart,
but those blind
to the ways of the world.

It's a struggle
between heart and soul
where the voices of one
clash against the needs
of the other
until all that is heard
is a noise
overpowering the song,
enveloping the notes
with chaos.

The frenzy is played out
again and again
on the dance floor
where the only thing
separating this moment
from the next
is the energetic flailing
of limbs

against the timed beat
heard.

Slowly,
the heat from pressed bodies
overwhelms everything else
until the scene fades
like a dream,
leaving only
the reality
that the dance is over
and the lights have faded
into daylight.

## 724. Untitled - 2002.07.15

The most beautiful times
in life
are at dawn and dusk
where the boundaries blur
and the veil between worlds
fades for that passing.

The retreating of moonlight
against the dusky pinks of
a sunrise
are mirrored by the
brilliant orange hues
that give way
to inky darkness.

In a never ending cycle
of light and dark,
there is no real separation
between the past
and the present,
nor between the
imagined and the real,
until everything blurs
into a fantasy once lived.

## 725. 2002.07.18

The first splashes of raindrops
against the steaming pavement
sizzle
with the heat.

This casual shower of summer
rain
is no relief
against the hot muggy weather
that envelopes the city.

Seeking shelter
in air-conditioned splendor,
the parched earth
swallows every droplet
in an unquenchable thirst.

Endless torrents of water drops
upon the land,
the cooling touch
leaves a scintillating sensation
upon the skin.

Wave after wave
the storm comes in,
pouring sheets of water
down cascading windows,
until all the world
is awash in liquid
satiation.

## 726. 2002.07.19

As the sun crosses the broken
horizon,
there is a lassitude
that fills the air,
the withdrawal of the searing
heat
that has consumed the day.

The cooling weather
is a welcome respite
to the hot sweat
and damp-filled day.

Watching the day fade away,
stretched out on a chaise-lounge
and sipping at cool refreshments,
a sigh of contentment is heard,
soft against the bustle
of the evening.

A simple breeze ruffles the grass
and serves as a silent
remembrance
of this passing
summer day.

## 727. 2002.07.20

It's big city living
that sees a bizarre combination
of crowded streets
but empty paths.

Where every person is hidden
behind air-conditioned splendor
and neighbors are
strangers to us all.

Only in the city centre
do remnants of a time past
still remain; where the streets
and shops are teeming with
people
wandering in and out.

Down by the Beaches,
the steady beats of jazz
float upon the summer breezes,
a sudden chant carrying
on the wind
to remind the skaters and riders
to pick up their ice cream
and errands
before the lake tides
come rushing into the sands.

As the day ends,
and people leave the sandy
shores,
life begins again
in lonely suburbia.

## 728. 2002.07.20

Who can describe despair
having never felt it?
Who can write of pain,
having never lived it?

Only living through
the depths of the hottest hells
could the strongest of souls
survive
to live another day.

It is survival
that governs the rules of the land,
where desperation drives everything
and strength is king.

Mental, physical, and emotional strength
to see past the surface
and visit the hope
that lingers within the eyes
of a young child,
to find shelter for the displaced,
and to give chances
for those without a break.

It is the downtrodden
and lost souls
that live within so many
of our inner cities;
where they live
forgotten
by those who would not know
of their fears
or their dreams
because we have not asked

how can we help?
but, instead turning a blind eye
to the homeless,
the poverty,
and the worldliness
that fills the eyes
of those too young
to dream of lost innocence.

## 729. Untitled - 2002.07.20

It's a hot, wet, blistering
afternoon
where the sun leaves
no place to hide,
and there is no relief
from the heat.

Ice cubes slide quickly
and disappear into slick shirts
and become one
with sweat-laden flesh.

There is no breeze
to take away the feeling
of heaviness in the air.

There are no cloud shadows
in the sky
to take shelter in,
nor are there shimmering oases
to lure us away
from the lurid thought
of more heat
during the day.

The height of summer
finds us seeking solace
in the endless supply
of cool crisp drops

that become a steady stream
upon parched lips.

The thought of a rain dance
is almost enough to cause a stir,
until reality sets in;
any more movement,
and truly,
all the clothing
will either stick forever,
or need to come off
immediately!

Daydreams of cold frozen treats
break into the time passing by,
reminding us again and again,
that a hot canvas
serves a need as well,
painting the surface
with cold points of contact,
followed by a steady stream of
slick sweetness,
the alternating sensations
gather in a coiled locus
and explode
in one breath
of ragged release.

# 730. 2002.07.21

There are none so blind
as those that would not see
the truth of life
as we live it.

Too often, we read of the woes
of many,
be they close
or be they far,
and mere talk
is never enough
to spur us to action,
beyond just thoughts,
and mere words.

Too often, our time is precious
even as we squander
in meaningless ways;
as our intent
is not enough
to transform to action.

Too easy
is it to not "see"
the problems that batter our
world;
too simple
to turn a cheek
and forget the whims of fate.

We are asked once more
to become the light of our world,
and live as the salt of our earth,
giving of time,
of care,
and of love,
to those that should not need to
ask.

## 731. 2002.07.21

The summer heat burns
in a slow blaze
against the ripe flesh
of peach gold.

As the rum soaks into
hardened surfaces,
everything takes on
a different haze ~
sweetened by time
and tempered by heat.

It is a slow burn
that gradually melts away
everything between
the top
and the hidden core,
until all that's left
is the red center
rigid to the touch.

Every bite sends a cascade
of juices
dripping down all sides,
eyes playfully watching
as the explosion of taste
overwhelms everything else.

Sharp nibbles
combined with a steady suction
yields fruity flesh
in a wild combination.

The last bites
end with a low hum
of happiness,
where the flush of red
has faded to pale pink.

## 732. 2002.07.22

Tongue tied,
watching as one after another
red globes
drop with lingering
lassitude
into dark depths
and waiting hunger.

Every bit splits into halves
with the easiest of times;
until everything is finally
vanquished,
and hunger is satiated once
more.

A sudden display
of agility
sees all fruits
swallowed whole;
puffed cheeks,
silent looks
yield naught,
except for the naked core,
and tied stem,
neatly wrapped
around one another.

## 733. 2002.07.22

As the hues darken from bright red
to dusk purple,
everything tightens
along a single point,
until it is ripe
beyond bursting.

Continued sunshine
sees a burst of freckles
across the top;
dimpling smooth flesh
once more.

Each bite
is a miniature explosion
of sensation
and taste
that melts across
yearning taste buds
like chocolate
on hot flesh.

The plumpness recedes
and gives way to soft flesh,
painted in hues
of red and orange;
like the sunset of a summers'
day.

## 734. 2002.07.22

A variance from large purple orbs
to small blue centers
draws the sweetness
from within.

Every splash of color
against pale white
casts an indelible mark forever.

Without hurry,
small globes cast themselves
willingly
into a creamy waterfall,
where they are covered
in milky white.

Every swallow
becomes a burst of elation,
senses reeling
from the contrast
between the sweet tang
and crisp cream.

## 735. 2002.07.23

As the weather cools,
and appetites diminish,
a mélange of colors pass this way,
sharply cut globes of varying hue,
honeyed yellow - crisp in taste
but yielding to a firm touch,
or pale orange - carrying
exotic tinges of sweetness.

Everything becomes drenched
into the slickest of sauces;
where honey does not compare;
every bite of stickiness
followed by a slight nibble;
all the juices become mixed
into an ambrosia not to be
found.

## 736. 2002.07.24

It's an endless
merry-go-round of words
that is fenced in
by a barrier of silence.

Intentions pave the road
to perdition
as time
paints no path
away from torment.

It's not the end of a moment
that is sought
but surcease
against the tidal wave
of words
that batter against
the barricade now.

## 737. 2002.07.26

To live the Way;
to bear the cross,
and to search for
hidden redemption.

Three words -
love one another,
tempered by three more -
do not judge.

To find forgiveness
in oneself,
to live life
and survive its revelations.

To seek shelter
in understanding,
to give grace
to all others.

To reflect in silence,
to sacrifice without mourning.

To be like the fire,
sharing light
and bring warmth
to one another.

## 738. 2002.07.27

In perfect love
and perfect trust,
the future of the world
gathered at one point
in time.

To renew their trust
and pledge their troth
to faith, love and fidelity.

To place their hopes
on lessons taught
from a past never forgotten,
but never truly learnt
in their lives.

In pure faith,
we send the makers of peace
on a mission
to tame the world,
to put aside the hate
and find
the love forgotten.

## 739. 2002.07.27

In G-d's love we live,
in divine grace we give.
In His goodness, we strive
to enrich each other's lives.

To find the good
and give the love,
go beyond the blood,
and feed the hope.

## 740. 2002.07.28

The skies were grey
so early in the morning,
heavy with anticipation
and raindrops.

A sea of humanity
making the walk together;
moving towards
a shared understanding.

The heavens open
in a flurry of raindrops
testing the resolve
of those gathered -
as the waiting
takes on a new focus.

A colorful carpet
of umbrellas,
greets those from up above,
heads bobbing in excitement.

As the Mass begins,
the storm abates
and the sunshine
peeks from behind.

An ocean of song
flows back into
the sea of faces.

Words of hope,
joy, and forgiveness
give the searching
pilgrims
one more unforgettable
memory to cherish.

## 741. 2002.07.29

What is the body
but a temple of G-d,
what is the soul
but an embodiment of hope?

To carry the world
and its hopes and dreams;
to entreaty for peace
in a time of war,
what is a man
but old and weary.

It is more than a meeting of
minds
between the young and old,
but a passing of the teachings
to the new generation.

From the static to the dynamic,
the youth will become
the leaders of the world;
and their hopes and faith
will lend credence in time.

Change from within
to change the outside;
it is so gradual as to be
nigh-invisible.

Three millennia of tradition
is a heavy tide to turn;
although civilizations
rise and fall
upon new ideas.

A new era begins
with the belief of
speaking the Truth,

and living the Truth.

Faith in Truth
brings light
to those who would wrought
false destruction.

## 742. 2002.07.29

There is a certain sanctity
in knowledge
that words attributed
to the unknown speaker
are no better
than those actions
by a coward.

Empty of meaning
but filled with vitriol,
their mere repetition
tolls the bell once more
on the icy descent
of silence.

Letting the absence of words
speaking their disdain,
and giving up
the empty feeling for today.

## 743. 2002.07.30

It's the road to perdition
when you try to become too
much.

Acceptance is not the final cost
but the last resort these days.

There is no pleasing the waves
that continually surge forward,
there is no relent against
the torrent of disdain
that rolls off
time after time.

Individuality within the
collective,
acceptance but with reluctance,
what is worth made of,
but the opinions of others,
what is the difference
between existence
and living
when everything passes
in a blur.

## 744. 2002.07.30

It's not about truth,
but image.
It's never truth that we see
but the facade that we expect.

There is no acceptance
because the whole is not
just the sum of parts.

There is no being,
just the pretending.

There is no journey
not defined by the end.


## 745. 2002.07.30

The trinity of words,
what forms the foundation
but the notion of love.

For oneself,
for others,
for G-d.

With love,
faith endures,
and hope lives.

With love,
dreams become real,
and lives become filled.

With faith,
we work towards
the hidden goal,
strengthened by knowledge,
bowed by gifts galore.

With hope,
we strive ever onwards,
unstinting in our belief
in the unfailing good
of others.


## 746. 2002.08.10

The dappled shade
provides cool comfort
in the heavy heat
that forms the beautiful summer
day.

The pastoral silence
is broken by
the sharp crack
of a drive onto the green.

White flags
are raised and lowered
in a regular pattern -
surrendering to no one
but one's self.

## 747. 2002.08.28

Sultry eyes and
ample lips
take their own sweet time
in a
slow caress that
fires all engines
and lingers in the
curling smoke;
tauntingly quiet
in a shifting
of the moment,
nape nipped by sharp teeth.


## 748. 2002.08.30

It's a strident voice
that bounces back
from the white walls
to an unending tirade -
a flow of words
that sift continuously
through the moments.

Fatigue sets in,
and numbness falls
like a snow-driven blanket
on the midwinter nights.

It's nothing again;
every time the flurry flies
like a river of words
into a sea of emptiness.


## 749. 2002.08.31

It's a silent cascade
of stolen moments
of peace and refuge
in the torrent
of white noise
that masks
as a bombardment
of snide comments
against the confusion.

Falling,
slipping, sliding,
into a miasma
of unfeelingness --
inured to the litany
of complaints
that form the foundation
of disdain and isolation.


## 750. 2002.09.05

In the early autumn haze,
the evenings cool quickly
after sunset.

A casual order
of changing leaves
drifting towards the end.

The crisp breeze
sends the flock of birds
scattering in sudden confusion.

## 751. 2002.09.09

when you fall to the bottom,
all you can do,
is look up.

to find something from
the depths
of despair,
to find yourself
once more.

hidden beneath
the surface,
beneath the fears
beneath the life,
is the self-knowledge
that masquerades
as self-hatred.

when you fall,
at the end you land,
be it on hard gravel
or soft sand.

when you fall,
reach out,
to find the reason
to climb.

every slow step
becomes a reason
to return
to hope once more.

## 752. 2002.09.11

It is unwanted knowledge
on the minds of the
unsuspecting
that destroys all the notions of
peace.

Each phrase
an utterance of hatred
and frustration
exploded.

Waiting for the tide
of anger
to wash against
the ceding shore,
until the waters break
once more.

## 753. 2002.09.12

The unrelenting tremors
that roll through
continue undiminished
in strength
or duration -
every pulsation
carrying
a wave
of painful emotion
unchanged.

The night hours
are broken
by the interminable pain -
cresting
in the darkest moments.

## 754. 2002.09.23

The midnight hour
marks a gradual slide
into the changing
of the seasons.

Hot summer heat
yields to autumn breezes
howling
along moonlit trails.

The dawn
sees both a pale yellow sun
and the round white moon
hung on separate ends
of the horizon.

The sunlight is deceptive
in warmth,
a sharp west wind
snapping us
into awareness.

The disappearing moon
is a remembrance
of a time past
filled with memories
of what once was.

## 755. 2002.10.12

An illicit pleasure ~
falling
through a haze
of clouds
into
a pool of sensation
that is the weakest
reflection
of the wave of
emotion
that cascades
from within.

Every moment
that passes
becomes
a mirror
of one another
until all
the points
converge
into one single
point
of
pain/pleasure.

## 756. 2002.10.14

Inner peace
from the release of outer desires.
The change is gradual
and covert in style.

A new thought begins
from the remnants of the past;
possibilities
becoming real once more.

Looking from the inside out,
or from the outside in,
the story changes
with each new moment.

Uncertain is the future,
but change is just a given
where fear is one part
of the process.

Hidden by the fear,
living by the knowledge
that the truth
begins with but a challenge.

## 757. 2002.10.15

To climb every mountain,
and cross every sea
without fear
or regrets --
true challenge is
also the knowledge
of when to let go
of the past
and the unchanging.

Energy best spent
in comfort
and knowledge
that efforts made
went beyond the mundane
into the realm
of the unbelieving.

Challenge
the status quo
to change it;
slow and subtle
are the nuances
where
transformations are made
until all that remains
is an empty chrysalis.

## 758. 2002.10.15

A monarch
resplendent in
in black and orange hues,
flies yearly
from tip to tip
as a challenge
from nature
to understand
the true meaning
of flight.

Realization becomes
reality
when the caterpillar disappears
in a death
of its own making,
to emerge
once more again
forever changed
into Nature's beauty.

## 759. 2002.10.22

On the streets,
between the sheets,
the white scrap of lace
floats gently
on the fall breeze
to land
on the sodden ground.

The silence not heard
is masked
by the sudden flurry
of shouts
as time after time,
people swerve
around this strip of whiteness,
so incongruous
once outside
that window.

## 760. 2002.10.30

It is the sweetest kiss
given under the pale moonlight
as the shadows shift
from limb to limb
of thread-bare trees
shorn of their silvery glow.

It is the haunting call
from the depths of the hallows
as the forest shifts
to reveal another world
of goblins and ghouls.

It is the stately dancing
of faerie Kings and Queens
as they hold court
in the late autumn evenings.

It is the cold wind blown
through the fallen leaves,
stirring the forgotten memories
on All Hallow's Eve.

## 761. 2002.10.30

Enter the night
where the chills run deep
into the bones
and the frost breath creeps
like an old hidden crone.

Venture into darkness
where the thoughts lie hidden,
and memories of the past
return unbidden.

Watch the flickering flames
waver against the wind,
a cold dance of joy
seen only in the mind.

The nightfall deepens
into midnight black,
where all the creatures hearken
to the hidden call to come back.

## 762. 2002.11.04

In the struggle
between love and honor,
there is a tenuous balance struck
between the here and now
and the past once lost.

Striving to forge a future
from the ashes of the
unforgiven,
searching for light
in a past of shadows,
finding love
in places unsought.

Above all that is held dear,
is the trust that
the truth that binds two souls
is set free.

## 763. 2002.11.25

Soft, slick, sweet sensation
gains intensity
from every moment,
running through shallow valleys
and around tight corners
until everything fades
to this very instant
of existence.

Tension merges
in silent need
until all that remains
is emptiness
fulfilled.

## 764. 2002.12.02

"I notice everything about you,"
and then turn around with a
grin.
So attention has been paid
with the subtlest of
compliments.

How could anything be
forgotten
to create an emptiness within
when the future becomes
a string of moments
captured in single pearls.

## 765. 2002.12.05

Slipping and sliding
amongst pure white
while the shouts of glee
fade into the distance.

Crunching and shuffling along
the city streets
catching the falling tears
of laughter.

Shivering and snuggling
in a nest of warmth,
enjoying the crackling fire,
the beauty of winter
filling all of one's' desire.

## 766. 2002.12.18

It's a circle of distance
that surrounds
the dark center.

It's the air of emptiness
that keeps
everything away.

It's the calculated silence
that mutes
the night air.

It's a deliberate knowledge
kept only
within.

## 767. 2002.12.24

It's a curious shift
of the pendulum
against the balance
of time.

There's a gradual change
in equilibrium
along the hidden lines.

From left to right,
near to far,
everything shifts
until all that remains
is the middle.

## ABOUT THE AUTHOR

Sometimes I string together words, and they may sound better than they appear on the page.

At other times, I enjoy the silence and simply watch the words draw forth.

Still better yet are the moments where the slightest effort nudge yields a waterfall of thoughts that tumble easily onto the page.

www.ingramcontent.com/pod-product-compliance
Lightning Source LLC
Chambersburg PA
CBHW060104230426

43661CB00033B/1418/J